WeightWatchers™
pure points™

READY IN
30 minutes!

over 60 recipes LOW IN POINTS

SIMON & SCHUSTER
A VIACOM COMPANY

Wendy Veale

First published in Great Britain by Simon & Schuster UK Ltd, 2000.
A Viacom Company.

Copyright © 2000

Simon & Schuster UK Ltd.
Africa House
64–78 Kingsway
London WC2B 6AH

Weight Watchers and *Pure Points* are trademarks
of Weight Watchers International, Inc. and used under its
control by Weight Watchers (UK) Ltd.

Photography: Steve Baxter
Styling: Marian Price
Food preparation: Wendy Lee
Design: Jane Humphrey
Typesetting: Stylize Digital Artwork
Printed and bound in Singapore

Weight Watchers Publications Manager: Elizabeth Egan
Weight Watchers Publications Executive: Corrina Griffin
Weight Watchers Publications Assistant: Celia Whiston

A CIP catalogue record for this book is available
from the British Library.

ISBN 0 743 20912 5

Pictured on the front cover: Mexican Beef Tacos, page 49
Pictured on the back cover: Baked Strawberry Alaska, page 58

contents

quick
& easy meals

Whether you are a busy parent with a demanding job running a home or a single person enjoying a hectic work and social calendar, life can be a whirlwind, in which days fade into months as the weeks rush by! Taking time out to take stock of everything seems like a dim and distant memory.

Even our eating habits have had to change to keep up with the times. What a great excuse for, well, finding an excuse! Skipping a meal, grabbing a take-away, finishing the kid's supper before rushing off to collect another tired and hungry soul. Sitting together over a meal and catching up on the day's events was once one of life's simple pleasures. Now it is too easy to for us all to sail from one ready meal to another like ships in the night.

WE CAN HELP...

So, life is a juggling act, and the thought of sticking to a diet as well as keeping several balls in the air is more of a challenge than ever before. That is why Weight Watchers constantly recognise the need to make sure its successful Programme continues to work, fitting around your life and not the other way round! Glance through this book and enjoy the prospect of spending less than 30 minutes to produce a fabulous meal for your family and friends to enjoy, whether it be mid-week suppers or casual entertaining at the weekends. All these delicious recipes will, with just a little planning, take the stress out of mealtimes. Quick and easy to prepare, you will find family favourites, like BBQ Bangers (great for a larger gathering), and portioned recipes too. For example, Cheesy Topped Turkey Steaks (page 33) can be made up, then popped under the grill on demand! Many dishes will happily keep warm without spoiling. Take advantage of the tips on how to freeze any leftovers so that you can have just one handy serving when you want it or make up double the quantity, where suitable for freezing, to enjoy whenever you fancy.

It is not easy to judge how the week will evolve as you fall out of bed on a Monday morning, but with a little planning, a shopping list which you stick to and a well stocked storecupboard, you can guarantee that whatever else the week has in store for you, there will be the time to enjoy nourishing, tasty Low Point food whether eating alone, or with family and friends.

Weight Watchers has taken time out just for you. You deserve it!

HINTS AND TIPS FOR SUCCESSFUL 30 MINUTE MEALS

Cooking

■ Use quick methods of cooking like grilling and stir-frying. And by using more tender, smaller cuts of meat, you will get great taste and hardly any waste.

■ Use just a few ingredients and keep down the number of cooking stages. Simple, good cooking with quality fresh ingredients requires little preparation and seasoning, and tastes the best.

■ Have a kettle of boiling water on stand-by to help speed up the cooking times!

■ Encourage the family to help with preparing meals. The recipes are simple to follow and willing helpers could make even lighter work – or not as the case may be!

Shopping

■ Plan and shop for your weekly menu in advance. This will save you time and help you to stay on the Programme with ease. It is also cost effective, resisting the temptation of unnecessary purchases!

■ Use the freshest available supply of fish. If you are lucky enough to have a travelling fishmonger, buy the fish from him on the same day that you want to cook it. Otherwise, buy fish in the supermarket and use it on the same day or freeze as necessary, according to the recommendations on the pack.

■ Buy foods which are in season since they offer the best value and flavour.

■ Ask your local butcher or fishmonger to prepare and individually vacuum pack chops, steaks and fillets for you to freeze. This can be far more cost effective and flexible than buying from the supermarket.

Preparing and Storing

■ Always keep a good stock of your favourite storecupboard ingredients, including your favourite ready-made sauces, relishes and soups. Refer to the useful list below.

■ Remember that with the recent demand for more additive-free ingredients, there is a shorter shelf-life for many fresh ingredients. Store produce and meats properly, and aim to use your fresh salads and vegetables first before you rely on frozen or canned substitutes.

■ Check the 'Best Before' dates on prepared foods. Select good buys which will be used or stored safely within the date.

■ Grow some fresh herbs in pots on the kitchen windowsill. These are available at supermarkets, and last for quite some time. This will allow you to have fabulous fresh flavours even in the depths of winter. In the warmer months, you can put the pots outside.

STORECUPBOARD ESSENTIALS

Fish: tuna in brine, salmon, anchovies, pilchards in tomato sauce

Fruit: canned pineapple, apricots, prunes, peaches, all in natural juice or apple juice, frozen raspberries and 'Fruits of the Forest' berries

Soups: Weight Watchers from Heinz varieties, Campbell's 99% fat-free condensed soups (mushroom, chicken, tomato) These are great as cook-in sauces

Pulses: Weight Watchers from Heinz Baked Beans in Tomato Sauce, butter beans, cannellini beans, chick-peas, red kidney beans

Tomatoes: sun-dried tomatoes, canned chopped tomatoes, canned chopped tomatoes with herbs, canned plum tomatoes, passata and purées, including sun-dried tomato purée

Vegetables: new potatoes, sweetcorn kernels, fresh peppers and canned pimentos, frozen peas, casserole mixes, stir-fry mixes

Pasta and Rice: there is a wide variety of pasta shapes and sizes which mean that the possibilities are endless for pasta dishes. Soup pasta such as vermicelli or small macaroni are ideal for bulking out soups. Basmati, Thai and Italian-style rice all have their own flavours and textures. Easy-cook American-style long grain white rice is a good accompaniment but the healthiest option is brown rice which takes quite a lot longer to cook

Oils, Vinegars and Mustards: look out for infused oils, flavoured mustards and speciality vinegars, particularly balsamic

Stock Cubes and Powder: Marigold Vegetable Stock Powder is especially good, cartons of ready-prepared fresh stocks freeze very successfully

Sauces: Tabasco, Worcestershire sauce, soy sauce, Weight Watchers from Heinz Salad Dressing, 95% fat-free salad dressings, Lea & Perrin's Root Ginger Sauce

Cook-In and Pour-Over Sauces: low-fat varieties such as 98% fat-free Homepride, tomato sauces and dried sauce mixes such as Schwartz and Colman's

Dried Herbs and Spices: jars of puréed chillies, garlic, ginger. Jars of lemon grass, pesto and harissa. Very convenient, but do remember that many are preserved in oil

Flours: plain flour, cornflour and sauce flour which dissolves easily and makes a lovely white sauce without the fat

Sicilian Country Soup: Easy parmesan crisps add a touch of sophistication to this lovely country soup

simple soups, salads &
suppers

These tasty meals are sure to make life a little easier. The soups are hot, comforting and filling and since most will freeze successfully, you can use them to plan ahead. The supper dishes and salads are ideal for a light meal and why not make up a fresh batch of salad dressing at the weekend to see you through a few days?

SICILIAN COUNTRY SOUP WITH PARMESAN CRISPS

POINTS

per recipe: 14   per serving: $3\frac{1}{2}$

Ⓥ if using vegetarian parmesan cheese

Serves 4

Preparation and cooking time: 25 minutes

Calories per serving: 235

Freezing: recommended

In an era of TV cooks and exotic travel, let's not overlook the simply delicious fresh flavours of a country vegetable soup. Adapt this hearty soup to use your favourite, seasonal vegetables.

600 ml (1 pint) hot vegetable stock

1 large onion, chopped

1 garlic clove, crushed

1 head of fennel or 2 small bulbs, outer layer(s) discarded, or 4 celery sticks

1 large carrot

2 courgettes

2 × 400 g cans of plum tomatoes

75 g ($2\frac{3}{4}$ oz) spaghetti, broken into short lengths

5 cm (2-inch) strip of orange rind, (optional, see Cook's Tips)

300 g can of cannellini beans, drained

125 g ($4\frac{1}{2}$ oz) fresh or frozen spinach

1 tablespoon fresh thyme (or 1 teaspoon dried)

2 tablespoons chopped fresh basil

salt and freshly ground black pepper

50 g ($1\frac{3}{4}$ oz) parmesan cheese, grated finely

1 Place the stock in a large pan, and bring to the boil. Meanwhile, put the onion, garlic, fennel, carrot and courgettes in a food processor and finely slice or chop them. Make sure that there is still some texture to the vegetables and that you don't just reduce them to mush. If you don't have a food processor, slice finely by hand but this will take longer. Then add the prepared vegetables to the boiling stock, cover and simmer for 10 minutes.

2 Stir in the tomatoes, spaghetti, orange rind if using, beans, spinach and thyme. Cover and continue to cook for 10 minutes.

3 Meanwhile preheat the grill to high. Using a non-stick baking tray or shallow frying pan, and a plain

6 cm ($2\frac{1}{2}$-inch) cutter as a template, make the cheese crisps. Place the cutter on a baking tray and sprinkle an even layer of cheese inside the cutter, to form a disc. Repeat with the remaining cheese, to make 8 crisps in total. You will need to do this in two batches. Place the tray under the grill to toast the cheese to a golden brown colour. This only takes a minute or so. Remove the tray and leave for a minute before carefully lifting each crisp onto a plate. Use a metal spatula to do this.

4 Season the soup to taste. Stir in the basil and ladle into bowls. Serve with the crisps on the side.

COOK'S TIPS Fennel has a distinct aniseed flavour and is a delicious but under-used vegetable. Choose 2 smaller bulbs rather than a large one, which may have tough outer layers.

The easiest way to get a 2-inch strip of orange rind is to use a potato peeler to gently peel off some rind.

VARIATION A teaspoon of chilli paste will add a touch of Sicilian heat. The Points will remain the same.

CHICKEN AND SWEETCORN CREOLE SOUP

POINTS	
per recipe: 10½	per serving: 2½

Serves 4
Preparation and cooking time:
25 minutes
Calories per serving: 330
Freezing: recommended

This tingling and spicy soup is a great introduction to using fresh chillies if you have never tried them before. Please note the Cook's Tip though!

2 onions, quartered
2 garlic cloves or 2 teaspoons garlic purée
1 red chilli, de-seeded
1 green pepper, de-seeded
850 ml (1½ pints) hot chicken stock
100 g (3½ oz) easy-cook rice
2 teaspoons ground coriander
500 g (1 lb 2 oz) chopped canned tomatoes or chunky passata (sieved tomatoes)
225 g (8 oz) cooked chicken breast, shredded
200 g can of sweetcorn kernels, drained
1 tablespoon chopped fresh oregano
salt

1 Use a food processor to roughly chop the onions, garlic, chilli and green pepper. You could also chop them by hand but this will take longer.
2 Pour the hot stock into a saucepan with the rice and bring to the boil. Add the prepared vegetables and the ground coriander. Season with salt.
3 Cover and simmer for 10 minutes, then stir in the canned tomatoes or passata, shredded chicken, sweetcorn and oregano.
4 Cover and cook for a further 5 minutes. Serve, piping hot.

COOK'S TIP Take great care when handling fresh chillies. Wash your hands thoroughly immediately after handling or better still, wear disposable gloves. If you should accidentally touch your eyes, bathe them with water.

WEIGHT WATCHERS TIP A swirl of low-fat plain yogurt is a delicious cooling garnish; 1 tablespoon per serving will not add any Points.

SPICY FISH SOUP

POINTS	
per recipe: 11	per serving: 2½

Serves 4 as a main meal soup
Preparation time: 10 minutes
Cooking time: 20 minutes
Calories per serving: 245
Freezing: recommended

Deliciously warm and welcoming on a chilly night, this soup is for the whole family to enjoy. If there is any left over, take it to work as a great midday 'pick me up'! Serve with crusty bread, adding the additional Points.

1 tablespoon vegetable oil
1 large onion, sliced finely
2 leeks, sliced finely
1 large carrot, grated
2 garlic cloves, crushed or 1 teaspoon garlic purée
1 teaspoon turmeric
1 teaspoon cumin
1 teaspoon garam masala
75 g (2¾ oz) red lentils
400 g (14 oz) canned chopped tomatoes
1.2 litres (2 pints) hot vegetable stock
400 g (14 oz) cod fillets, cut into chunks
juice of 2 limes
2 tablespoons chopped fresh coriander
salt

1 Add the oil to the pan and fry the onion, leeks, carrot and garlic for 2–3 minutes. Add the spices and lentils and stir-fry for a further minute. Stir in the tomatoes and hot stock. Bring to the boil, then cover and simmer for 15 minutes.
2 Add the fish, lime juice and coriander, and continue to cook with the lid on for a further 5 minutes. Check the seasoning. Ladle into deep bowls.

COOK'S TIP If you have one, use the slicing attachment on a food processor to make swift work of preparing the vegetables.

VARIATION Replace the cod with a 200 g can of tuna in brine (drained) and 200 g (7 oz) cooked prawns. The Points per serving will be 3.

ORIENTAL CHICKEN NOODLE SOUP

POINTS

per recipe: 9½   per serving: 4½

Serves: 2 as a main meal soup
Preparation and cooking time:
25 minutes
Calories per serving: 285
Freezing: not recommended

For those of us who enjoy a taste of the exotic, help is at hand since so many new ingredients are now widely available.

1.2 litres (2 pints) hot chicken stock
1 garlic clove, chopped or 1 teaspoon garlic purée
1 stick of lemongrass, trimmed and sliced paper thin
1 teaspoon Lea & Perrin's Root Ginger Sauce or ½ level teaspoon of ground ginger
2 x 150 g (5½ oz) skinless chicken breast, cut into strips
1 red chilli, de-seeded and chopped
75 g (2¾ oz) shiitake or button mushrooms, sliced
4 spring onions, halved lengthways and cut into 5 cm (2-inch) strips
50 g (1¾ oz) medium egg noodles
1 tablespoon Thai fish sauce
4 tablespoons chopped fresh coriander

1 Pour the hot stock into a large saucepan. Add the garlic, lemon-grass and ginger. Cover and simmer.
2 Meanwhile dry-fry the chicken in a non-stick pan for 5 minutes. Add the chilli, mushrooms and spring onions, and stir-fry for a further 5 minutes.
3 Drop the noodles into the simmering stock and cook for 3–4 minutes. Add the chicken mixture and the fish sauce. Heat through to allow the flavours to mingle. Stir in the coriander. Serve.

COOK'S TIP Garlic, chilli, lemon grass and ginger are all available ready prepared in small glass jars. Once opened, they will keep in the refrigerator for up to 6 weeks.

VARIATIONS Strips of lean beef, pork or 300 g (10½ oz) fresh prawns are all a delicious substitute for chicken. The Points per serving will be 5 for beef, 3 for pork and 4 for prawns.

HAM, LEEK AND POTATO SOUP

POINTS

per recipe: 7   per serving: 1½

Serves 4
Preparation and cooking time:
30 minutes
Calories per serving: 145
Freezing: recommended

This is a wonderfully wholesome soup, ideal for those 'hungry' Saturday lunchtimes when you are never quite sure how many family or friends might pop by.

2 leeks
2 medium potatoes, peeled and quartered
600 ml (1 pint) hot vegetable stock
1 tablespoon cornflour
200 ml (7 fl oz) semi-skimmed milk
2 teaspoons Dijon or wholegrain mustard
2 tablespoons chopped fresh parsley (or 2 teaspoons dried)
150 g (5½ oz) wafer-thin smoked ham
salt and freshly ground black pepper

1 Slice the leeks and potatoes finely or use the fine slicing blade on a food processor. Transfer to a saucepan, pour over the hot stock, cover and cook for 10 minutes.
2 Meanwhile, blend the cornflour with the milk. Stir in the mustard and parsley. Add to the potato and leeks, stirring until the mixture thickens slightly. Simmer for a further 10 minutes.
3 Cut the ham into pieces and add to the saucepan. Season to taste. Heat gently for another minute or two before serving.

VARIATIONS Replace the ham with wafer-thin turkey, and substitute the parsley with 1 tablespoon of chopped fresh tarragon or sage. The Points per serving will be the same.

**Ham, Leek and Potato Soup:
A delicious and comforting soup**

WARM POTATO AND MACKEREL SALAD

POINTS	
per recipe: 13	per serving: 6½

Serves 2
Preparation and cooking time:
25 minutes
Calories per serving: 490
Freezing: not recommended

Salads served warm or at the very least, at room temperature, are more flavoursome than when eaten chilled. Try this salad and see!

250 g (9 oz) new potatoes, quartered
200 g (7 oz) French beans, trimmed
½ red onion, sliced into rings
1 celery stick, chopped finely
4 cocktail gherkins in vinegar, drained and halved lengthways
2 teaspoons grated horseradish
150 ml (5 fl oz) Yogurt and Herb Dressing (see page 13)
150 g (5½ oz) smoked mackerel fillets, flaked into large pieces
8 cherry tomatoes, whole, or 2 large tomatoes, quartered
salt and freshly ground black pepper
iceberg salad leaves, to serve

1 Cook the potatoes in boiling water for 10–15 minutes, or until tender and 5 minutes before the end, add the green beans. Drain and toss in the onion, celery and gherkins.
2 Mix the grated horseradish into the Yogurt and Herb Dressing, and fold into the potato mixture. Season.
3 Arrange the mackerel and tomatoes on a bed of crisp salad leaves. Spoon over the warm potato salad and serve.

COOK'S TIP Make sure you don't use a creamed horseradish, which has a higher fat content.

VARIATION Replace the mackerel with 150 g (5½ oz) canned tuna in brine, drained. The Points per serving will be 1.

COURGETTE, FETA AND CHICK-PEA SALAD

POINTS	
per recipe: 24½	per serving: 6

Ⓥ if using vegetarian feta cheese
Serves 4
Preparation and cooking time:
10 minutes
Calories per serving: 315
Freezing: not recommended

1 tablespoon olive oil
1 red onion, sliced thinly
3 courgettes, sliced
400 g (14 oz) canned chick-peas, drained
150 ml (5 fl oz) Tomato, Garlic and Balsamic Vinaigrette (see page 12)
200 g (7 oz) feta cheese, diced
salt and freshly ground black pepper
salad leaves, to serve

1 Heat the oil in a frying pan and stir-fry the onion and courgette over a high heat for 3–4 minutes or just long enough to lightly colour without softening too much.
2 Transfer to a bowl, add the chick-peas and the dressing. Leave to cool to room temperature.
3 Add the cheese and mix gently. Adjust the seasoning, to taste. Serve on a bed of salad leaves.

WEIGHT WATCHERS TIP If you want to bulk out the salad with more vegetables, add blanched green beans or additional courgette, and chunks of tomato.

TANDOORI CHICKEN SALAD

POINTS	
per recipe: 10	per serving: 2½

Serves 4
Preparation time: 10 minutes
Calories per serving: 195
Freezing: not recommended

It's quicker to make use of ready-flavoured chicken breasts.

450 g (1 lb) cooked tandoori chicken pieces
225 g (8 oz) tomatoes, de-seeded and chopped
6 spring onions, sliced
2 green chillies, de-seeded and chopped finely
2 tablespoons chopped fresh coriander
200 ml (7 fl oz) Creamy Yogurt and Herb Dressing (see page 13)
salt and freshly ground black pepper
salad leaves, to serve

1 In a large bowl, toss the chicken with the tomatoes, spring onions, chillies and coriander.
2 Toss the chicken mixture with the Yogurt and Herb Dressing. Season.
3 Arrange the salad leaves on plates and spoon the chicken on top.

Tandoori Chicken Salad: Naan bread is an excellent accompaniment to this spicy salad; just remember to count the Points.

TOMATO, GARLIC AND BALSAMIC VINAIGRETTE

POINTS

per recipe: ½

Makes 150 ml (¼ pint)
Preparation time: 10 minutes
Calories per recipe: 90
Freezing: not recommended

2–3 large ripe tomatoes, skinned

2 garlic cloves, crushed or 1 teaspoon garlic purée

2 tablespoons sherry vinegar or red wine vinegar

1 teaspoon balsamic vinegar

2 teaspoons sun-dried tomato paste

½ teaspoon caster sugar

2 tablespoons chopped fresh herbs (e.g. mint, basil or chives)

salt and freshly ground black pepper

1 De-seed the tomatoes. Use a sieve to catch the seeds and then press the juice into a food processor or liquidizer. Add the tomatoes, garlic, vinegars, tomato paste and sugar. Process to a smooth dressing and add the herbs. Season well.

2 Transfer to a covered container and refrigerate until required. Serve at room temperature.

VARIATIONS Add 1 de-seeded green chilli or ½ teaspoon harissa (Moroccan chilli paste) for a fiery hot dressing. Bart Spices do a ready-prepared harissa which you will find beside the spices in the supermarket.

Tomato, Garlic and Balsamic Vinaigrette; Orange and Chive Dressing; Honey and Mustard Dressing; Warm Potato and Mackerel Salad with Creamy Yogurt and Fresh Herb Dressing (top to bottom left to right): so many different low Point ways to dress a salad!

HONEY AND MUSTARD DRESSING

POINTS

per recipe: 4

Ⓥ *Makes 150 ml (¼ pint)*
Preparation time: 5 minutes
Calories per recipe: 130
Freezing: not recommended

Now a classic, this light, delicate dressing is delicious tossed into salad leaves, or a potato salad. It's also very tasty with grilled meats, chicken and oily fish.

| 100 ml (3½ fl oz) low-fat plain yogurt |
| 2 teaspoons runny honey |
| 2 teaspoons whole-grain mustard |
| 1 teaspoon Dijon mustard |
| salt |

1 Mix all the ingredients well. Season to taste.

COOK'S TIP Choose a sharp low fat plain yogurt to contrast well with the honey.

VARIATION Add 1 teaspoon of lemon or orange zest for a fruity dressing. Experiment with other flavoured mustards which you'll see in most major supermarkets.

CREAMY YOGURT AND FRESH HERB DRESSING

POINTS

per recipe: 1

Ⓥ *Makes 150 ml (¼ pint)*
Preparation time: 5 minutes
Calories per recipe: 65
Freezing: not recommended

Use a 0% fat Greek-style yogurt as the base for this creamy dressing. Add some fresh, vivid green herbs and you have an instant dressing or dip for a whole array of recipes. Try it with Courgette, Feta and Chick-pea Salad (page 10) and Greek-style Lamb Kebabs (page 45).

| 150 g (5½ oz) 0% fat Greek-style yogurt |
| juice of 1 lime |
| 1 tablespoon chopped fresh parsley |
| 1 tablespoon chopped fresh chives |
| 1 tablespoon chopped fresh mint |
| ½ teaspoon Dijon mustard |
| freshly ground black pepper |

1 Mix all the ingredients together. Transfer to a covered container and chill until required.

COOK'S TIP The longer you leave the dressing to chill, the more the flavour develops.

VARIATIONS If a salad recipe lends itself to a strong minty dressing, for example, simply add an extra tablespoon of mint and reduce the other herbs accordingly.

To make this recipe into a dip, halve the lime juice and add 2 finely chopped spring onions. Serve with crunchy vegetables or with grilled meats. This dip is ideal with the Mexican Beef Tacos (page 49).

ORANGE AND CHIVE DRESSING

POINTS

per recipe: 2

Ⓥ *Makes 150 ml (¼ pint)*
Preparation time: 10 minutes
Calories per recipe: 145
Freezing: not recommended

Try this tangy dressing tossed through salad leaves, plain hot rice or couscous. The flavours are a perfect match with grilled fish and chicken too.

| juice of 1 large orange (about 100 ml/ 3½ fl oz) |
| zest of ½ orange |
| ½ teaspoon Dijon mustard |
| 1 tablespoon finely chopped fresh chives |
| 1 tablespoon low-fat plain yogurt |
| 2 teaspoons olive oil |
| salt and freshly ground black pepper |

1 Whisk all the ingredients together and season to taste.
2 Transfer to a covered container and chill until required.

COOK'S TIP Use this dressing as a baste for grilled or barbecued meats, chicken and fish.

VARIATION Replace the orange with lemon for a zesty dressing. Add 1 teaspoon runny honey, to sweeten. The Points will remain the same.

SQUASH AND BLUE CHEESE RISOTTO

POINTS

per recipe: 20   per serving: 10

V   Serves 2

Preparation and cooking time:
30 minutes
Calories per serving: 695
Freezing: not recommended

An interesting array of squashes have been appearing in the supermarkets over the last couple of years, and are becoming more fashionable to cook with. This is the ideal recipe for those of you who have yet to try this interesting vegetable.

2 teaspoons olive oil

1 large onion, chopped

2 celery sticks, chopped

450 g (1 lb) winter squash or pumpkin, skinned, de-seeded and cut into 1 cm (¹/₂-inch) cubes

200 g (7 oz) Italian-style easy-cook rice

600 ml (1 pint) hot vegetable or chicken stock

4 sage leaves, torn or ¹/₂ teaspoon dried

2 tomatoes, de-seeded and diced

75 g (2³/₄ oz) low-fat soft cheese with garlic and herbs

a handful of chopped fresh parsley

50 g (1³/₄ oz) blue cheese, crumbled

salt and freshly ground black pepper

1 Heat the oil in a large saucepan, and gently cook the onion and celery until softened. Add the squash or pumpkin and cook for 2 more minutes.

2 Stir in the rice and add the hot stock. Cover and simmer for 10–15 minutes, until the stock is nearly absorbed.

3 Stir in the sage, tomatoes, soft cheese and parsley. Season, to taste. Divide between the individual bowls, and crumble over the blue cheese.

COOK'S TIP Arborio is the classic short stubby grain used to give risotto its creamy consistency. It does, however, require more cooking than the easy-cook Italian-style rice. This is an acceptable 'cheats' version.

WEIGHT WATCHERS TIPS Omit the oil and dry-fry the vegetables to save 1 Point per serving. Replace the low-fat soft cheese with virtually fat-free fromage frais and save 1 Point per serving.

RED HOT LEGS

POINTS

per recipe: 10   per serving: 2¹/₂

Serves 4
Preparation and cooking time:
25 minutes
Calories per serving: 170
Freezing: recommended

These red hot chicken legs are great.

8 medium chicken drumsticks, skinned

1 teaspoon garlic purée

4 tablespoons tomato ketchup

1 tablespoon clear honey

1 tablespoon Dijon mustard

1 teaspoon fresh chilli paste or

¹/₂ teaspoon chilli powder

a dash of Worcestershire sauce

salt

TO SERVE

onion rings

lemon wedges

1 Place the drumsticks in a shallow flameproof dish. Mix together the garlic, tomato ketchup, honey, mustard, chilli paste or powder and Worcestershire sauce; season with salt. Pour the sauce over the drumsticks, coating them thoroughly.

2 Preheat the grill to medium. Cook the drumsticks for 15–20 minutes, turning frequently, until tender.

3 Serve hot, with the lemon wedges and fresh onion rings.

COOK'S TIP The recipe suggests raw onion rings but if you don't like raw onion, pop them under the grill for a few moments while the drumsticks are cooking.

WEIGHT WATCHERS TIPS Serve these drumsticks with bowls of celery strips, tomato wedges and crisp green pepper chunks. There are lots of 'free' Points to nibble at with the chicken. If you have the time, make some coleslaw; otherwise buy a 95% fat-free ready-prepared one. Remember to add the extra Points.

Red Hot Legs:
Have plenty of
finger bowls
and serviettes
ready as you
enjoy these
fabulous
drumsticks!

TUNA AND CAULIFLOWER CHEESE

Serves 4
Preparation and cooking time:
20 minutes
Calories per serving: 210
Freezing: recommended

Here's a fishy twist to the tale – a classic family favourite with the addition of canned tuna. Serve with freshly cooked green vegetables or a crisp salad.

1 cauliflower, broken into large florets

2 × 185 g cans of tuna in brine, drained

75 g (2¾ oz) half-fat Cheddar or Edam cheese, grated

15 g (½ oz) freshly grated parmesan cheese

FOR THE SAUCE

25 g (1 oz) sauce flour

450 ml (16 fl oz) skimmed milk

½ teaspoon Dijon mustard

salt and freshly ground black pepper

1 Cook the cauliflower in a saucepan of boiling water for 10 minutes, until just tender.

2 Meanwhile, make the sauce. Put the flour in a small saucepan, gradually whisk in the milk and bring to the boil, whisking continuously. Reduce the heat and simmer for a minute until it thickens. Stir in the mustard, and season to taste.

3 Preheat the grill. Fold the tuna and half-fat cheese into the sauce. Fold in the cauliflower florets.

4 Spoon into a shallow gratin dish. Sprinkle on the parmesan cheese, and grill for 3–4 minutes, until toasted golden. Serve.

Tuna and Cauliflower Cheese: An ideal supper for the family, ready in only 20 minutes!

MARMITE AND BACON RICE

Serves: 2
Preparation and cooking time:
20 minutes
Calories per serving: 435
Freezing: not recommended

125 g (4½ oz) easy-cook rice

1–2 teaspoons Marmite, dissolved in 4 tablespoons hot water

4 tablespoons frozen peas

1 small onion, sliced

75 g (2¾ oz) lean back bacon

2 eggs, beaten

chopped fresh parsley or chives, to garnish

1 Cook the rice according to the pack instructions. Then stir in the dissolved Marmite and the peas. Cover and leave to stand on the hob.

2 Dry-fry the onion and bacon in a non-stick frying pan, until the onion is soft and tinged golden, and the bacon is crispy.

3 Pour the eggs into the frying pan, and stir constantly over a medium heat for 2–3 minutes to slowly scramble them.

4 Stir into the cooked rice and the Marmite. Sprinkle on the parsley. Serve, piping hot.

HERBY DROP SCONES WITH CHAR-GRILLED VEGETABLES

POINTS

per recipe: 10½   per serving: 2½

(V) Serves 4

Preparation and cooking time:
25 minutes
Calories per serving: 215
Freezing: not recommended

As a child, I used to love Scotch Pancakes, fresh from the griddle, in time for tea. Times have moved on and now I can enjoy a modern, savoury version with a continental twist. I wonder what my mother would think…!

100 g (3½ oz) self-raising flour
4 tablespoons chopped fresh herbs e.g. chives, oregano, basil (or 1 teaspoon dried)
1 egg, beaten
150 ml (¼ pint) skimmed milk
1 yellow pepper, de-seeded and sliced into rings
2 courgettes, sliced diagonally
low-fat cooking spray
2 large tomatoes, sliced thickly
100 g (3½ oz) low-fat mozzarella cheese, sliced
8 fresh basil leaves
salt and freshly ground black pepper

1 Place the flour, herbs, egg, milk and seasoning in a liquidizer or food processor and blend to a stiff batter. Leave to stand.

2 Heat a non-stick frying pan and dry-fry the pepper and courgettes, until just softened and turning golden. Remove from the pan. Preheat the grill to medium.

3 Lightly spray the frying pan with oil. Add the batter in large tablespoons and cook until bubbles appear on the surface. Flip over the scones and cook the other side until golden. Keep warm in a clean tea towel while you cook the remaining batch, to make 8 scones in total.

4 Place a couple of slices of courgette, a ring of pepper, a tomato slice and a mozzarella slice on each scone. Grill until the cheese is melted and golden. Season well with ground black pepper. Serve, topped with a fresh basil leaf.

WEIGHT WATCHERS TIP
Replace the cheese with 8 wafer-thin slices of Parma ham, frazzled until crisp. The Points will remain the same.

THE BIG BRUNCH

POINTS

per recipe: 5½   per serving: 5½

Serves 1

Preparation and cooking time:
15 minutes
Calories per serving: 385
Freezing: not recommended

Why not spoil yourself over a leisurely weekend Brunch? It will set you up for the day! And it's a really relaxed way of entertaining.

1 teaspoon vegetable oil
150 g (5½ oz) canned cooked potatoes or leftover boiled potatoes, sliced thickly
½ small onion, sliced thinly
75 g (2¾ oz) cooked beetroot, chopped into small pieces
50 g (1¾ oz) thick slice of cooked ham, cut into strips
1 egg, poached
1 tablespoon half-fat crème fraîche
½ teaspoon horseradish relish

1 Heat the oil in a small frying pan. Fry the potatoes and onion over a high heat until browned. Stir in the beetroot and ham and gently heat through for 5 minutes.

2 Poach the egg until lightly set. Mix together the crème fraîche and horseradish.

3 Spoon the potato mixture on to a hot plate. Top with the poached egg and drizzle on the dressing. Serve.

COOK'S TIP This makes a tasty supper dish too.

VARIATIONS Replace the ham with sliced chicken or turkey breast. Smoked haddock fillet (100 g/3½ oz) is delicious, too. The Points per serving will be 5½ with chicken, 6 with turkey and 5 with haddock.

fabulous fish

Fish is an excellent ingredient for Weight Watchers. It's low in Points but high in protein and minerals. Oily fish, in particular, is an excellent source of essential fatty acids which are thought to offer protection against heart disease.

If you don't regularly cook fish, there's lots of help at hand in the supermarkets at the superb wet fish counters. They are happy to give advice and sell anything from the smallest fillet to the biggest catch of the day! Just ask!

Grilled Cod with a Caribbean Salsa: The differing flavours and textures of feisty salsa and simple cod make a fantastic taste combination.

GRILLED COD WITH A CARIBBEAN SALSA

POINTS	
per recipe: 7½	per serving: 2

Serves 4
Preparation and cooking time:
20 minutes
Calories per serving: 145
Freezing: not recommended

Liven up a plainly grilled cod steak with this feisty salsa. The opposing flavours and textures are surprisingly good together. And be sure to use fresh pineapple for a superb flavour! This dish is delicious served with mashed sweet potato, just remember to add the Points. Courgettes and green beans go well, too.

4 × 150 g (5½ oz) cod steaks or fillets
1 teaspoon vegetable oil
FOR THE SALSA
1 small red onion
1 green chilli, de-seeded
1 red pepper, de-seeded and quartered
a handful of basil leaves
juice of 2 limes
2 tomatoes, de-seeded and diced finely
2 pineapple rings, cut into 5 mm (¼-inch) dice
salt

1 To make the salsa, finely chop the onion and chilli in a food processor, until they are almost like a purée and then add the red pepper and basil leaves. Take care to make sure that you only process them lightly so that the red pepper is still a little chunky.
2 Stir in the lime juice, tomatoes and pineapple. Season with salt. Cover and leave to one side.
3 Brush the cod steaks with a little oil. Cook under a medium grill for 3–4 minutes on each side or until tender.
4 Spoon the salsa on to the grilled cod and enjoy!

COOK'S TIP The Bird's Eye Chilli is pretty hot, so do take the usual care when handling fresh chillies (see Chicken and Sweetcorn Creole Soup, Cook's Tip, page 8).

VARIATIONS Replace the cod with fresh tuna steaks or medium chicken breast fillets. The Points per serving will be 3 for both chicken and tuna.

PRAWNS WITH CHICK-PEAS AND CORIANDER

POINTS

per recipe: 10	per serving: 5

Serves 2
Preparation and cooking time:
25 minutes
Calories per serving: 365
Freezing: not recommended

2 teaspoons olive oil

1 onion, halved and sliced thinly

1–2 garlic cloves, chopped, or 1–2
teaspoons garlic purée

1 small red chilli, de-seeded and
chopped, or 1 teaspoon fresh chilli
paste

Plaice Rolls with a Minty Pea Purée: The vibrant colours and flavours evoke a warm summer's day.

400 g (14 oz) canned, chopped
tomatoes with herbs

4 tablespoons dry white wine

2 teaspoons light soy sauce

2 teaspoons tomato purée

400 g (14 oz) canned chick-peas,
drained

175 g (6 oz) prawns, defrosted if frozen

4 tablespoons chopped fresh coriander

salt

1 Heat the oil in a saucepan and
cook the onion for 5 minutes until
softened and lightly coloured. Add
the garlic and chilli and cook for a
further minute.

2 Add the tomatoes, wine, soy sauce
and tomato purée. Simmer, covered,
for 5 minutes.

3 Stir in the chick-peas and prawns.

Heat through for 3–4 minutes. Season,
to taste. Stir in the coriander. Cover
and remove the pan from the heat.
Leave to stand for 5 minutes to allow
the coriander flavour to infuse.

WEIGHT WATCHERS TIP Omit
the oil and wine, add an extra 200 g
(7 oz) canned chopped tomatoes,
and cook all the ingredients at stage
1 and 2 together for 10 minutes,
or until the onions are soft. Then
proceed to stage 3. This will add
5 minutes and save you 1 Point.

VARIATION Replace the prawns
with 175 g (6 oz) cod fillet, cut into
chunks. Add at stage 3, and cook
for 5 minutes. The Points per serving
will be 4½.

PLAICE ROLLS WITH A MINTY PEA PURÉE

POINTS

per recipe: 13½	per serving: 3½

Serves 4
Preparation and cooking time:
25 minutes
Calories per serving: 160
Freezing: not recommended

This is delicious with new season
baby potatoes and carrots. Add the
additional Points for the potatoes.

225 g (8 oz) frozen peas

10–12 fresh mint leaves

4 tablespoons low-fat plain yogurt

8 plaice fillets (about 550 g/1 lb 3 oz
in total)

2 tablespoons lemon juice

2 teaspoons mint jelly

salt and freshly ground black pepper

1 Cook the peas and refresh under
cold running water. Process to a
coarse purée together with the mint
and 2 tablespoons of yogurt. Season
to taste.

2 Divide the filling between the fillets,
roll up and arrange on their ends, in
a frying pan. (The rolls need to fit
snugly.) Pour in just enough boiling
water in to cover the base of the pan.
Add the lemon juice. Cover tightly
with foil and poach for 10 minutes,
or until the fish turns opaque.

3 Transfer the fish to warm plates,
reduce the liquid in the pan to 4
tablespoons. Whisk in the mint jelly
and remaining yogurt. Season to
taste. Drizzle over the plaice rolls.
Serve.

COOK'S TIP Replace the mint
jelly with mint sauce, if you prefer.

STIR-FRY SALMON AND BROCCOLI WITH GINGERED RICE

POINTS

per recipe: 7½   per serving: 7½

Serves 1

Preparation and cooking time:
15 minutes

Calories per serving: 550

Freezing: not recommended

This recipe is very good for when I am cooking just for myself, and so versatile. It is important to pamper yourself when eating alone!

50 g (1¾ oz) easy-cook rice

1 carrot, grated

2 teaspoons Lea & Perrin's Root Ginger Sauce or 1 teaspoon grated fresh root ginger

1 teaspoon sesame oil

½ red pepper, de-seeded and cut into strips

100 g (3½ oz) broccoli florets

1 teaspoon garlic purée

a few drops of Tabasco sauce

2 spring onions, sliced

125 g (4½ oz) salmon fillet, cut into strips

1 teaspoon fish sauce (optional)

1 teaspoon soy sauce

1 Cook the rice according to the pack instructions. Drain and stir in the carrot and ginger sauce. Cover and keep warm.

2 Meanwhile, heat the oil in a non-stick frying pan or wok. Add the pepper and broccoli and stir-fry over a high heat for 2 minutes. Add the garlic, Tabasco and spring onions. Stir-fry for a further minute.

3 Add the salmon, fish sauce, if using, and soy sauce. Cook for 2 minutes, then serve on the bed of rice.

COOK'S TIP Orange goes well with both salmon and ginger, so for a special occasion, add the segments of a small orange to the rice, just before serving.

VARIATION Chicken, turkey and pork strips all work well in place of salmon, just omit the fish sauce. The Points per serving will be 3 for chicken, 6½ for turkey and 6 for pork.

SMOKED MACKEREL HOTPOTS

POINTS

per recipe: 29½   per serving: 7½

Serves 4

Preparation and cooking time:
20 minutes

Calories per serving: 400

Freezing: not recommended

I like to make it in individual ramekins – there is something special about having your very own portion! Serve with baby new potatoes and peas, adding the necessary Points.

1 teaspoon vegetable oil

1 small onion, chopped finely

2 celery sticks, chopped

1 courgette, chopped

350 g (12 oz) smoked mackerel fillets, skinned and flaked

4 tomatoes, de-seeded and chopped

juice of ¼ lemon

4 tablespoons low-fat soft cheese

25 g (1 oz) fresh breadcrumbs

25 g (1 oz) half-fat Cheddar cheese, grated

salt and freshly ground black pepper

1 Heat the oil in a saucepan and fry the onion, celery and courgette for 5 minutes. Remove from the heat. Stir in the flaked mackerel and tomatoes.

2 Blend together the lemon juice and soft cheese. Season with salt and pepper, then fold into the smoked mackerel.

3 Either divide the mixture between four 10 cm (4 inch) ramekins or spoon into an 850 ml (1½ pints) shallow flameproof dish. Preheat the grill to a medium setting.

4 Mix together the crumbs and cheese and spread evenly over the surface of the mackerel mixture.

5 Grill for 4–5 minutes, or until the crumbs are golden and the cheese is bubbling. Serve.

Smoked Mackerel Hotpots: The ideal savoury supper.

SEAFOOD KEBABS WITH A CHILLI LIME GLAZE

POINTS

per recipe: 13½   per serving: 3½

Serves 4
Preparation and cooking time
15 minutes
Calories per serving: 235
Freezing: not recommended

Succulent and meaty, cod and salmon are a popular choice, and are readily available pre-packed. Serve with rice and salad or green beans.

450 g (1 lb) cod fillet, cut into 2.5 cm (1-inch) chunks

300 g (10½ oz) salmon fillet, cut into 2.5 cm (1-inch) chunks

1 garlic clove, crushed, or 1 teaspoon garlic purée

2 teaspoons fresh hot chilli paste

juice of ½ lime

8 cherry tomatoes or 4 small tomatoes, halved

1 lime, cut into quarters

chopped fresh coriander, to garnish

1 Place the fish in a plastic bag. Mix together the garlic, chilli and lime juice. Add to the fish, twist the bag to seal, and gently shake the bag to coat the fish with the marinade.

2 Divide the cod, salmon, tomatoes and lime wedges into four groups and then thread a selection from each group on to one of the four skewers. Preheat the grill to high. Place a piece of foil on the grill rack.

3 Use any remaining glaze to brush the kebabs, and then grill for 3–4 minutes on each side, or until the fish becomes opaque.

4 Serve garnished with coriander.

COOK'S TIP Prepare some easy-cook rice to eat with the kebabs. Add a few strands of saffron or a pinch of turmeric for a colourful yellow rice. Add 1½ Points per 75 g cooked portion.

VARIATION For a special occasion, replace some or all of the cod with 225 g (8 oz) each of scallops and tiger prawns (peeled and de-veined). The Points per serving will be 4.

CAJUN MACKEREL FILLETS WITH CRISPY SWEET VEGETABLES

POINTS

per recipe: 15   per serving: 7½

Serves 2
Preparation and cooking time:
20 minutes
Calories per serving: 485
Freezing: not recommended

Oily fish, such as mackerel, trout and sardines, are highly nutritious and contain essential fatty acids believed to provide protection against heart disease. They are also a good source of Vitamin D so, ideally, they should be included on your shopping list every week. Here is a tasty, quick recipe to encourage the habit!

2 mackerel fillets, skin on (about 175g/ 6 oz each)

½ teaspoon Cajun seasoning (e.g. Schwartz)

2 shallots, quartered

1 small green or red pepper, de-seeded and cut into chunks

2 small carrots

2 small courgettes

1 tablespoon soy sauce

1 tablespoon soft brown sugar

1 tablespoon rice vinegar or cider vinegar

1 tablespoon tomato ketchup

1 Heat a non-stick frying pan. Sprinkle the skinless side of the mackerel with the seasoning. Place seasoned side down, in the hot pan. Cook for 2–3 minutes over a moderate heat. Turn the pieces over and cook for a further 2–3 minutes or until the fish flakes easily and is slightly charred.

2 Remove from the pan and keep warm. Add the shallots, pepper and 4 tablespoons of water to the pan. Cook for 3 minutes, shaking the pan frequently. Use a potato peeler to slice the carrots and courgettes into ribbons. Add to the pan together with the remaining ingredients. Stir-fry for 2 minutes.

3 Serve the mackerel with the crunchy vegetables.

COOK'S TIP Rice wine vinegar is a slightly sweet and mildly acidic vinegar, popular in Asian cookery. Use it in vinaigrettes for a much lighter flavour.

VARIATIONS Replace the mackerel with trout or salmon fillets. The richness of the oily fish works well with the sweet and sour vegetables. The Points per serving will be 5 with salmon and 4 with trout.

Seafood Kebabs with a Chilli Lime Glaze: Choose your favourite fish for these deliciously spicy kebabs.

Fisherman's Pot: Be sure to include the feathery tops of the fennel since they add such a lovely flavour.

FISHERMAN'S POT

POINTS

per recipe: 16   per serving: 4

Serves 4
Preparation time: 5 minutes
Cooking time: 25 minutes
Calories per serving: 295
Freezing: recommended

Choose the best fresh fish available for this tasty catch! Delicious served with puréed broccoli or fresh green beans.

1 head of fennel, sliced thinly (optional)
450 g (1 lb) new potatoes, cut into quarters
a strip of orange or lemon rind
1 tablespoon chopped fresh dill, tarragon or chives (or 1 teaspoon dried)
600 ml (1 pint) hot vegetable stock
4 tablespoons white wine
225 g (8 oz) salmon fillets, cut into 8 chunks
225 g (8 oz) haddock fillets, cut into 8 chunks
4 tablespoons half-fat crème fraîche
salt and freshly ground black pepper

1 Place the first five or six ingredients in a saucepan, cover and bring to the boil. Simmer for 15–20 minutes or until the vegetables are tender.
2 Add the chunks of fish and cook for 3 minutes. Stir in the crème fraîche. Season to taste.

COOK'S TIP For puréed broccoli, simply cook until tender, then process in a liquidiser until smooth. Season well.

WEIGHT WATCHERS TIP This recipe is ideal for entertaining, as the preparation is minimal and it needs little attention during cooking. However, for an everyday meal, you may want to omit the crème fraîche and wine. This will save you a ½ Point.

VARIATION Use a bag of stir-fry vegetables for sheer convenience, instead of the cabbage and baby corns. Although they are available fresh, a frozen bag is a good standby in the freezer. You can use as little as you need without any waste.

SMOKED HADDOCK FLORENTINE WITH A CHIVE SAUCE

POINTS

per recipe: 5   per serving: 2½

Serves 2
Preparation and cooking time: 25 minutes
Calories per serving: 225
Freezing: not recommended

A healthy alternative to the classic haddock and spinach combination.

2 × 150g (5½ oz) un-dyed smoked haddock fillets, skinned
1 shallot or ½ small onion, chopped
250 g (9 oz) fresh baby spinach
1 tomato, de-seeded and diced
4 tablespoons half-fat crème fraîche
2 tablespoons chopped fresh chives
salt and freshly ground black pepper

1 Bring a frying pan, half filled with water, almost to the boil, then add the smoked haddock with the shallot or onion and poach gently for 4–5 minutes.
2 Meanwhile, rinse the spinach and remove any tough stalks, then put it into a saucepan, with the water still clinging to the leaves. Cover and cook for 3–4 minutes until it is wilted. Drain well in a colander. Season to taste.
3 Arrange the spinach between two hot plates and place a drained fish portion on top. Scatter the chopped tomato over each serving. Keep warm under the grill, on a low setting.
4 Spoon 6 tablespoons of the fish liquor into a small pan. Boil rapidly, to reduce to 2 tablespoons, add the crème fraîche and the chives. Season with pepper. Spoon over the haddock. Serve.

COOK'S TIPS Naturally smoked haddock develops an even yellow hue whereas when artificial dyes are applied they only give a vivid yellow colour on the surface of the fish. Very fresh smoked fish can be frozen for a maximum of 3 months, but do check with your fishmonger that the fish hasn't previously been frozen.

WEIGHT WATCHERS TIP If you have enough Points, poach an egg to serve on top of the haddock. This will add 1½ Points per serving.

VARIATIONS Use salmon fillets instead of haddock, and basil in place of chives as an alternative. The Points per serving will be 5.

chicken & turkey

To make life easier for us all and to help us put together tasty and healthy meals more quickly, the supermarkets now offer us a huge choice of individual cuts and pre-packs of chicken and turkey which all make light work of the time spent preparing tasty food. Turkey is now available all year round and is an excellent meat when you are trying to lose weight since it is low in Points but very flavourful.

ORANGE MUSTARD CHICKEN WITH PARSNIP MASH

POINTS

per recipe: 5   per serving: 5

Serves 1
Preparation and cooking time:
25 minutes
Calories per serving: 300
Freezing: recommended

2 medium parsnips, peeled and sliced thinly
1 × 150 g (5½ oz) boneless, skinless chicken breast
1 teaspoon coarse-grain mustard
2 teaspoons reduced-sugar orange marmalade
1 tablespoon low-fat fromage frais
1 teaspoon chopped fresh chives or parsley
salt and freshly ground black pepper

1 Preheat the grill to medium/hot. Cook the parsnips in a saucepan of boiling water for 15 minutes or until tender.
2 Meanwhile, place the chicken, upper side face down, in a foil-lined grill tray. Season with salt and pepper. Grill for 8–10 minutes, then turn the chicken over and spread on the mustard and marmalade. Cook for a further 8–10 minutes or until the chicken is tender, and the glaze has turned a deep golden colour.
3 Drain the cooked parsnips. Mash with the fromage frais and chopped chives or parsley. Slice the chicken and serve piled on top of the mash.

COOK'S TIP There is a wonderful selection of mustards to look out for. It's a good idea to keep one or two varieties handy in the store cupboard.

CHICKEN AND POTATO MASALA

POINTS

per recipe: 21½   per serving: 5½

Serves 4
Preparation and cooking time:
25 minutes
Calories per serving: 270
Freezing: recommended

Masala simply means 'spiced' and is an Arabic word which means 'interest' or 'necessities'. Luckily, using a ready-prepared sauce means that we don't need a long list of ingredients to make this recipe interesting and just delicious.

2 onions, sliced thinly
450 g (1 lb) skinless chicken breast, cubed
4 tablespoons medium Masala curry paste (e.g. Sharwood's)
400 g (14 oz) canned, chopped tomatoes
200 g (7 oz) mushrooms, halved
550 g (1 lb 3 oz) canned new potatoes, drained and halved
200 ml (7 fl oz) boiling water
2 tablespoons chopped fresh coriander
salt

1 Dry-fry the onions and chicken in a non-stick pan for 5 minutes. Stir in the curry paste and the tomatoes. Mix well, and add the mushrooms, potatoes and boiling water. Cover and simmer for 10 minutes.
2 Stir in the chopped coriander. Check the seasoning, to taste.

Spicy Mango Chicken Pancakes: See how easily leftover chicken can be transformed into a quick and incredibly tasty meal.

SPICY MANGO CHICKEN PANCAKES

POINTS

per recipe: 25½   per pancake: 4

Makes 6 pancakes

Preparation and cooking time:
25 minutes

Calories per pancake: 255

Freezing: not recommended

Serve with a crisp green salad.

127 g pack of pancake batter mix

1 teaspoon vegetable oil

1 egg

450 g jar of Homepride 98% fat-free
Creamy Curry Sauce

450 g (1 lb) cooked chicken, chopped

1 ripe mango, chopped

2 spring onions, chopped

3 firm tomatoes, sliced

1 Make the pancake batter according to the pack instructions, adding the egg. Wipe, as required, a dab of oil around the inside of a small non-stick omelette pan and make 6 pancakes. Wrap the cooked pancakes in foil and keep warm under a low grill setting.

2 Gently heat the Madras sauce in a saucepan and add the cooked chicken. Heat thoroughly, stirring, until piping hot.

3 Fold in the mango pieces and spring onion. Divide the filling between the pancakes. Fold into neat squares, and arrange on a foil-lined grill pan. Top each pancake with slices of tomato.

3 Heat through under the grill until the tomatoes are lightly cooked and the pancakes are hot.

SPEEDY COQ AU VIN

POINTS

per recipe: 14½   per serving: 3½

Serves: 4

Preparation time: 10 minutes

Cooking time: 15 minutes

Calories per serving: 220

Freezing: recommended

Serve with mashed potato and green beans (French, of course!), adding the extra Points as necessary.

6 shallots, halved

450 g (1 lb) boneless chicken breast, cubed

100 g (3½ oz) lean smoked bacon, diced

200 g (7 oz) button mushrooms

425 ml (¾ pint) hot chicken stock

150 ml (¼ pint) full-bodied dry red wine

2 teaspoons Worcestershire sauce

1 tablespoon chopped fresh thyme (or 1 teaspoon dried)

salt and freshly ground black pepper

a few thyme sprigs, to garnish

1 Pour some boiling water over the shallots, to cover, and leave for 5 minutes. This makes them very easy to peel – and without tears! Meanwhile, dry-fry the chicken and the bacon in a non-stick saucepan for 3 minutes, stirring frequently.

2 Add the mushrooms and the shallots to the chicken, together with a couple of tablespoons of stock. Cook briskly for 2 minutes, then reduce the heat and pour on the remaining stock and wine.

3 Stir in the Worcestershire sauce, thyme and a little seasoning, to taste. Cover and simmer for 15 minutes. Garnish with thyme sprigs and serve.

THAI GREEN CHICKEN WITH COCONUT SAUCE

POINTS

per recipe: 14½   per serving: 7

Serves 2
Preparation and cooking time:
15 minutes
Calories per serving: 355
Freezing: not recommended

Green curry paste is a delicious
blend of green peppers, green
chillies, lemon grass, coriander,
fish sauce, garlic and lime juice.

75 g (2¾ oz) easy-cook rice
225 g (8 oz) broccoli, broken into
small florets
50 g (1¾ oz) sugar snap peas or green
beans, trimmed

225 g (8 oz) skinless chicken breast,
cut into strips
4 spring onions, chopped
2 tablespoons Thai green curry paste
100 ml (3½ fl oz) reduced-fat
coconut milk
1 tablespoon chopped fresh coriander
salt, to taste

1 Cook the rice according to the
pack instructions.
2 Meanwhile, cook the broccoli in a
small saucepan of boiling water for
5 minutes. Add the peas or beans
and cook for a further 2 minutes.
Make sure however that the
vegetables still have some 'bite'.
3 Dry-fry the chicken strips in a
non-stick pan until golden. Stir in the
spring onions and curry paste, and
cook for a further minute. Add the
drained vegetables, coconut milk and
coriander. Heat gently, combining
the ingredients. Season with salt,
to taste.
4 Serve the curry on a bed of rice.

COOK'S TIP If you have ever
wondered what the difference is
between red and green curry paste,
red curry paste is milder and sweeter.

WEIGHT WATCHERS TIP Look
out for the reduced-fat coconut milk
(Bart Spices and Amoy now both do
one) – a must when cooking Thai
food the Weight Watchers way! If
you have any coconut milk left over,
simply freeze it in ice cube trays, and
then pop out 2 cubes per serving for
an instant curry.

FRUITY CHICKEN COUSCOUS

POINTS

per recipe: 12½   per serving: 6

Serves 2
Preparation and cooking time:
25 minutes
Calories per serving: 460
Freezing: not recommended

Couscous is a staple throughout
North Africa but has now become
a popular grain in Europe. In 'hot'
pursuit is harissa, a fiery paste of
chilli pepper and garlic, used in
Moroccan and Tunisian cooking.

180 g (6½ oz) canned apricot halves,
drained, natural juice reserved
200 ml (7 fl oz) vegetable or chicken
stock

½ teaspoon ground coriander
½ teaspoon Madras curry powder
125 g (4½ oz) couscous
1 small carrot, grated
1 small courgette, grated
200 g pack of cooked chicken breast
fillets
1 teaspoon harissa (e.g. Bart's)
15 g (½ oz) toasted, flaked almonds
flat leaf parsley, to garnish

1 Chop the apricots and set aside.
In a small pan bring the stock, with
the spices, to the simmering point.
Remove from the heat, stir in 3
tablespoons of the reserved apricot
juice, the couscous, carrot and
courgette. Cover and leave for 5
minutes to absorb the liquid.
2 Now score the cooked chicken
fillets with a sharp knife, and rub in
the harissa. Heat the chicken up,
either by following the pack
instructions for the microwave, or
placing them under a medium hot
grill for 4–5 minutes.
3 Stir the apricots and almonds into
the couscous with a fork. Divide
between 2 plates, and arrange the
hot chicken on top. Garnish with
parsley.

WEIGHT WATCHERS TIP This
is really delicious served with a mint,
cucumber and low-fat yogurt raita.
There are no Points for 1 tablespoon
of low-fat plain yogurt. Or try one
of the dressings on page 13 drizzled
over the chicken.

Fruity Chicken Couscous: Now it's easy to recreate the subtle and sensual flavours of the Middle East.

Lemon-Glazed Turkey with Mange-Tout Peas: Enjoy the classic combination of lemon and honey in this sweet and savoury dish.

LEMON-GLAZED TURKEY WITH MANGE-TOUT PEAS

POINTS

per recipe: 4½   per serving: 2

Serves 2

Preparation and cooking time:
15 minutes

Calories per serving: 180

Freezing: not recommended

Serve, sizzling, stuffed into pitta bread pockets with loads of crisp salad leaves, or with plain boiled rice, adding the Points as necessary.

225 g (8 oz) turkey breast strips (look out for stir-fry packs or escalopes)

125 g (4½ oz) mange-tout peas, trimmed

2 spring onions, sliced

1 tablespoon clear honey

juice of ½ lemon (2 tablespoons)

1 tablespoon chopped fresh basil leaves

1 teaspoon sesame seeds

salt and freshly ground black pepper

1 Briskly dry-fry the turkey in a non-stick frying pan over a high heat for 3–4 minutes until the meat is well sealed and lightly coloured.

2 Add the mange-tout peas and spring onions with 1 or 2 tablespoons of water if needed and stir-fry for a further 3–4 minutes. Add the honey, lemon juice, chopped basil and sesame seeds. Season well.

3 Let the juices come to the boil, coating the turkey with the glaze that is forming. Serve immediately.

CHEESE-TOPPED TURKEY STEAKS

POINTS

per recipe: 16   per serving: 8

Serves 2

Preparation and cooking time:
25 minutes

Calories per serving: 265

Freezing: not recommended

2 turkey breast steaks (each about 125 g/4½ oz)

50 g (1¾ oz) half-fat Cheddar cheese, grated

25 g (1 oz) fresh breadcrumbs

1 small Cox or Granny Smith apple, peeled and cored

2 walnut halves, chopped coarsely

a pinch of dried sage

salt and freshly ground black pepper

1 Place the steaks between two sheets of greaseproof paper, and flatten them out to approximately 15 mm (⅝-inch) thick. (This helps speed up the cooking time, and gives the impression of a larger portion!) Preheat the grill.

2 Mix together the cheese, breadcrumbs, apple, nuts and sage. Season to taste.

3 Line the grill pan with foil. Grill the turkey steaks for 4–5 minutes on each side. Spread the topping mixture evenly over each steak. Continue to cook for a further 2–3 minutes, until the cheesy breadcrumb mixture turns golden brown. Serve.

CHINESE TURKEY SKEWERS WITH NOODLES

POINTS

per recipe: 32   per serving: 8

Serves 4

Preparation and cooking time:
25 minutes

Calories per serving: 405

Freezing: not recommended

3 tablespoons soy sauce

1 tablespoon tomato purée

1 teaspoon sweet chilli sauce

2 teaspoons caster sugar

150 ml (¼ pint) hot chicken stock

450 g (1 lb) turkey breast fillets, cut into strips lengthways

250 g (9 oz) packet of medium egg noodles

½ Chinese cabbage, shredded

100 g (3½ oz) baby corns or asparagus tips, trimmed

1 Preheat the grill to high. Mix together the soy sauce, tomato purée, chilli sauce and sugar. Put half of this into a small pan with the stock. Add the turkey to the remaining sauce, and coat well. Thread the turkey on to four skewers and grill for 6–8 minutes, turning occasionally, until cooked.

2 Meanwhile, break the noodles into a large pan of boiling water. Add the cabbage and baby corns or asparagus tips. Bring to the boil, then cover and simmer for 4 minutes.

3 Heat through the sauce in the pan.

4 Drain the noodles and vegetables, then return to the pan, pour on the warmed sauce and toss to coat thoroughly. Divide between four, and place a kebab on top.

TURKEY AND BROCCOLI PASTA WITH MUSTARD CRÈME FRAÎCHE

Serves 4
Preparation and cooking time:
25 minutes
Calories per serving: 305
Freezing: not recommended

You can use any dried pasta you may have on hand for this quick supper dish. I like broken-up spaghetti – possibly because it takes longer to eat!

175 g (6 oz) dried pasta e.g. fusilli, tagliatelle or spaghetti

275 g (9¹/₂ oz) broccoli florets

275 g (9¹/₂ oz) turkey breast strips

1 small onion, chopped

125 g (4¹/₂ oz) mushrooms, sliced

200 ml (7 fl oz) hot chicken stock

1 tablespoon Dijon mustard

2 teaspoons cornflour

4 tablespoons half-fat crème fraîche

salt and freshly ground black pepper

1 Cook the pasta in a large pan of boiling and slightly salted water for 10 minutes. Halfway through, add the broccoli, and cook for the remaining 5 minutes.

2 Meanwhile, dry-fry the turkey, onion and mushrooms for 3–4 minutes in a large non-stick frying pan. Pour on the hot stock. Bring to the boil, then stir in the mustard and cornflour, blended with the crème fraîche. Simmer for 5 minutes.

3 Thoroughly drain the pasta and broccoli. Combine with the turkey and sauce. Season well, with plenty of black pepper. Divide between warmed bowls and serve.

WEIGHT WATCHERS TIP Crème fraîche is a pasteurised thick, French soured cream. Although it contains less fat than double cream it adds lots of body (and unwanted pounds!) to sweet and savoury dishes. So imagine the whoops of delight when a 'half fat' alternative was launched!

VARIATION Add a teaspoon of garlic purée to the turkey at stage 2.

SIZZLING TURKEY WITH SWEET POTATO AND PINEAPPLE

Serves 4
Preparation and cooking time:
20 minutes
Calories per serving: 285
Freezing: recommended

America introduced us to the potato, tomato, turkey, chilli, and the pineapple, not forgetting chocolate. Here is a sweet and spicy supper dish to salute their great discoveries! This is delicious eaten with spinach or green beans.

500 g (1 lb 2 oz) sweet potatoes, peeled, sliced and quartered

450 g (1 lb) minced turkey

1 large onion, chopped

2 teaspoons hot chilli powder

2 teaspoons fresh ginger purée

227 g can of pineapple chunks in natural juice

1 small red pepper, de-seeded and diced

1 teaspoon cornflour

salt

chopped fresh coriander, to garnish

1 Cook the sweet potatoes in boiling salted water for 10 minutes. Meanwhile, dry-fry the turkey and onion in a non-stick saucepan until the turkey becomes crumbly and lightly coloured. Add the chilli powder and ginger and cook for a further minute.

2 Drain the pineapple, reserving the juice. Drain the potatoes. Add the pineapple and the potatoes to the minced turkey with the red pepper. Cover and cook over a gentle heat for 5 minutes.

3 Blend the pineapple juice with the cornflour. Stir into the saucepan and cook for a further minute or until the juice has thickened. Season to taste. Serve.

COOK'S TIP Sweet potatoes are now widely available and can be recognised by their reddish-purple skins and elongated, irregular shape. They are often used in Caribbean cooking and add a vivid orange colour and rich sweet flavour to dishes.

WEIGHT WATCHERS TIP Invest in some small plastic containers, or wash and save your low-fat spread cartons. They are perfect for freezing individual portions of left over food. You will then always have an exciting frozen menu to choose from!

Pork with Tomatoes and Red Wine: This is the perfect recipe to make in large quantities and freeze in handy portions for future impromptu meals.

meat in minutes

Glance through this chapter for lots of quick recipe ideas using meat. You can forget the clock, and messy roasting tins, as these recipes make the best of quality cuts of tender beef, lamb and pork which are ideally suited to quick methods of cooking. More taste and less washing up!!

PORK WITH TOMATOES AND RED WINE

POINTS

per recipe: 10   per serving: 2½

Serves 4
Preparation time: 10 minutes
Cooking time: 20 minutes
Calories per serving: 220
Freezing: recommended

Serve with rice and fresh vegetables, adding extra Points for the rice.

350 g (12 oz) pork tenderloin or fillet, cut into strips

1 large onion, chopped
400 g (14 oz) canned chopped tomatoes with herbs
150 ml (¼ pint) red wine
1 tablespoon tomato purée
150 ml (¼ pint) hot vegetable or chicken stock
1 teaspoon dried herbes de Provence or Italian mixed herbs
225 g (8 oz) chestnut or open-cap mushrooms, halved
2 courgettes, sliced thickly
1 teaspoon herbes de Provence or Italian Seasoning
2 teaspoons cornflour
salt and freshly ground black pepper

1 Dry-fry the pork and onion for 5 minutes, then stir in the canned tomatoes, red wine, tomato purée, stock, herbs, mushrooms, courgettes and sage. Bring to the boil, then cover and simmer for 15 minutes.
2 Blend the cornflour to a paste with just enough water and stir in to the pork mixture. Simmer uncovered, for 1–2 minutes to thicken the sauce. Season to taste. Serve.

COOK'S TIP Bulk this out for the family with additional chopped vegetables such as carrots, celery, and leeks for a hearty and filling casserole.

PORK FILLET WITH BUTTER BEANS

POINTS

per recipe: 13   per serving: 3

Serves 4
Preparation and cooking time: 20 minutes
Calories per serving: 185
Freezing: not recommended

275 g (9½ oz) pork fillet, cut into 5 mm (¼-inch) slices
2 teaspoons cornflour
300 ml (½ pint) skimmed milk
4 teaspoons coarse-grain mustard
425 g (15 oz) canned butter beans, drained and rinsed
2 plum tomatoes, de-seeded and sliced thinly

1 tablespoon chopped fresh chives
salt and freshly ground black pepper

1 Dry-fry the pork for 5 minutes.
2 Blend the cornflour with the milk and mustard. Add to the pork and cook, stirring, until the sauce thickens. Season to taste.
3 Carefully mix in the butter beans, tomatoes and chives. Simmer for 3–4 minutes before serving.

WEIGHT WATCHERS TIP
Replace the butter beans with 225 g (8 oz) fresh broad beans, (particularly when they are in season) and 125 g (4½ oz) button mushrooms, sliced thinly. Add both at the end of stage 1, dry-frying for 2 minutes. This will reduce the Points per serving to 2½.

VARIATION Stir in 4 tablespoons of half-fat crème fraîche at stage 3. Add ½ Point per serving.

Pork Fillet with Butter Beans: Something really filling for the end of the day!

Pork and Piccalilli Escalopes with Apple Mash: Pork offers excellent value, both for your Points and your purse.

PORK AND PICCALILLI ESCALOPES WITH APPLE MASH

POINTS

per recipe: 8½   per serving: 4

Serves 2
Preparation and cooking time:
30 minutes
Calories per serving: 310
Freezing: not recommended

Now here is a pickle that has stood the test of time! A vivid crunchy vegetable relish that usually makes an appearance at Christmas time! The potato and apple mash is a delicious accompaniment.

1 large potato (about 275 g/9½ oz), sliced thinly

1 small Bramley apple

2 medium lean pork steaks (about 100 g/3½ oz each)

2 tablespoons piccalilli

1 teaspoon chopped fresh chives

salt and freshly ground black pepper

1 Cook the potato slices in boiling water for 10 minutes until tender. Peel and slice in the apple. Cover the saucepan and leave to stand for 5 minutes.

2 Meanwhile dry-fry the pork for 3 minutes on each side. Add the piccalilli and 4 tablespoons of water. Stir briskly to blend the ingredients. Season to taste.

3 Drain and crush the potatoes and apple. Stir in the chives and season to taste. Serve the pork and piccalilli pan juices with the mash.

WEIGHT WATCHERS TIP Look for lean cuts of pork such as stir-fry strips, steaks, escalopes, mince and fillet.

Chinese Pork Parcels: Oriental and exotic but very quick and easy to make.

CHINESE PORK PARCELS

POINTS

per recipe: 20   per serving: 5

Serves 4
Preparation and cooking time:
20 minutes
Calories per serving: 315
Freezing: not recommended

Try this nifty way with minced pork for an economical mid-week meal.

100 g (3½ oz) easy cook rice

450 g (1 lb) minced pork

2 fresh garlic cloves, chopped or 2 teaspoons garlic purée

1–2 teaspoons puréed ginger

2 tablespoons soy sauce

4 spring onions, trimmed and chopped

200 g bag of beansprouts

1 large carrot, grated

1 iceberg lettuce, whole leaves separated, to serve

freshly ground black pepper

1 Cook the rice according to pack instructions.

2 Dry-fry the minced pork in a large frying pan for 5 minutes until lightly coloured and crumbly. Stir in the garlic and ginger and cook for a further 5 minutes to ensure the pork is well done.

3 Stir in the soy sauce, spring onions, beansprouts, carrot and pepper. Cook for 2–3 minutes.

4 Drain the rice, and stir into the pork. Arrange two whole lettuce leaves on each plate. Divide the mince mixture between them, roll each leaf up and enjoy with additional soy sauce, for dipping.

BBQ BANGERS

POINTS

per recipe: 27½   per serving: 7

Serves 4
Preparation time: 10 minutes
Cooking time: 15 minutes
Calories per serving: 230
Freezing: recommended for the sauce

Comfort food at its best! This BBQ sauce is delicious with sausages, but it's also wonderful with chicken drumsticks and lamb cutlets. Serve with mustard-flavoured mashed potato or a baby baked potato and some peas or cabbage, adding the Points as necessary.

450 g (1 lb) half-fat sausages

salt and freshly ground black pepper

FOR THE SAUCE

1 small onion, grated

½ green pepper, de-seeded and diced

1 tablespoon Worcestershire sauce

1 tablespoon redcurrant jelly

1 teaspoon red wine vinegar

1 teaspoon brown sugar

300 ml (½ pint) passata (sieved tomatoes) or tomato juice or chopped canned tomatoes

2 teaspoons cornflour

1 Cook the sausages under a medium grill for 12–15 minutes.
2 Meanwhile, make the sauce. Simply place all the ingredients except the cornflour in a small saucepan and heat, stirring, until the ingredients are well combined.
3 Blend the cornflour to a smooth paste with a little cold water. Stir into the sauce and bring to a gentle boil, until thickened. Season to taste.
4 Serve the sausages with the sauce poured over.

COOK'S TIP Look out for passata which is now widely available in all the major supermarkets. It is a rich pulp of tomatoes and you can also buy it with added herbs and garlic.

STOVED SAUSAGES AND SPUDS

POINTS

per recipe: 15½   per serving: 4

Serves 4
Preparation time: 10 minutes
Cooking time: 20 minutes
Calories per serving: 300
Freezing: recommended

Save time at the start of the week by cooking extra potatoes over the weekend to use in this hearty hotpot – a delicious supper to start off the week!

2 onions, sliced thickly

450 g (1 lb) 95% fat-free pork sausages, cut into pieces

750 g (1 lb 10 oz) canned cooked potatoes (or any leftover potatoes)

300 ml (½ pint) hot chicken stock

25 g (1 oz) half-fat Cheddar cheese, grated finely

salt and freshly ground black pepper

1 Dry-fry the onions and the sausages in a flameproof frying pan or shallow cast iron dish for 4–5 minutes or until lightly browned. Use a slotted spoon to transfer 2 tablespoons of the onions to a saucer. Transfer the remaining sausage mixture to a bowl.
2 Slice the potatoes and arrange half of them in the bottom of the frying pan. Season and then top with the sausage mixture. Pour on the stock and then top with a layer of the remaining potatoes. Scatter with the reserved onions and cheese.
3 Cover and cook gently for 15 minutes, then grill for 4–5 minutes until the onions are crisp and the cheese is bubbling. Serve.

COOK'S TIP If you want to use freshly cooked potatoes, slice thinly and cook in boiling water for 10 minutes, at stage 1.

WEIGHT WATCHERS TIP This recipe uses 95% fat-free sausages but you can also use half-fat sausages. Just remember to add 2 Points per serving.

VARIATION Quorn sausages, vegetable stock and a vegetarian cheese can easily be used to make this recipe suitable for vegetarians. The Points per serving will be 5.

**Glazed Sausage
Kebabs:
Perfect for
an impromptu
summertime
barbecue.**

GLAZED SAUSAGE KEBABS

Makes 8 kebabs
Preparation time: 10 minutes
Cooking time: 15 minutes
Calories per kebab: 135
Freezing: not recommended

---

450 g (1 lb) 99% fat-free sausages,
each cut into 3

2 courgettes, sliced thickly

8 small tomatoes, halved

2 dessert apples, cored, quartered and
cut into eighths

4 small onions, quartered

FOR THE GLAZE

2 tablespoons mango chutney

2 tablespoons orange juice

1 tablespoon coarse-grain mustard

½ teaspoon ground ginger

1 To make the glaze, gently heat all the ingredients together in a small pan.
2 Heat the grill to medium. Thread the sausages, courgettes, tomatoes, apples and onions alternatively on to eight small metal skewers.
3 Grill the kebabs for 12–15 minutes, turning and brushing them with the glaze. Mix any pan juices with any left over marinade and dribble this over the kebabs.

COOK'S TIP Soak wooden skewers in water first to prevent them from catching fire.

VARIATION Replace the apples with chunks of pineapple or apricot halves and use the natural juice from the cans instead of the orange juice in the glaze. Adjust the Points if necessary.

GRILLED GAMMON WITH A PINEAPPLE CRUST

Serves 4
Preparation and cooking time:
20 minutes
Calories per serving: 220
Freezing: not recommended

I love this combination of ingredients. It's delicious with peas and grilled tomatoes, adding extra Points for the peas.

---

4 × 125 g (4½ oz) gammon steaks,
trimmed

2 canned pineapple rings, drained
and diced

1 spring onion, chopped finely

25 g (1 oz) fresh white breadcrumbs

25 g (1 oz) parmesan cheese, grated
finely

1 teaspoon English mustard

1 Cook the gammon steaks under a medium grill for 4 minutes on each side.
2 Meanwhile, mix together the pineapple and spring onion with the breadcrumbs and cheese.
3 Spread each steak with a little mustard and the pineapple crumb mixture. Return to the grill for a further 2 minutes or until the crumbs become golden and crisp.

Grilled Gammon with a Pineapple Crust: Parmesan cheese has such a lovely strong flavour that you only need a little for a fabulous taste.

SOMERSET SAUSAGE CASSEROLE

POINTS

per recipe: 19½ per serving: 5

Ⓥ *if using vegetarian sausages*

Serves 4
Preparation time: 10 minutes
Cooking time: 20 minutes
Calories per serving: 280
Freezing: recommended

Delicious with rice or pasta but remember to add the extra Points.

450 g (1 lb) half-fat sausages
2 medium leeks, sliced
2 celery sticks, sliced
2 carrots, sliced thinly
1 green pepper, de-seeded and sliced

400 g (14 oz) canned, chopped tomatoes with herbs
1 tablespoon tomato purée
150 ml (¼ pint) dry cider
1 tablespoon cornflour
175 g (6 oz) open mushrooms, sliced
1 tablespoon chopped fresh sage (or 1 teaspoon dried)

1 Dry-fry the sausages in a saucepan for 2–3 minutes, turning frequently. Add the leeks, celery, carrots and pepper slices. Cover and cook, shaking the pan every now and then, for a further 2–3 minutes.
2 Pour on the tomatoes, purée and cider. Bring to the boil, then cover and simmer for 10 minutes. Blend the cornflour with 3 tablespoons of water, and stir into the casserole together with the mushrooms and sage. Simmer, uncovered, for a further 10 minutes.
3 Season to taste.

COOK'S TIP Don't forget to make good use of your food processor for speedy chopping and slicing vegetables if you have one.

WEIGHT WATCHERS TIP Replace the cider with apple juice. The Points will remain the same.

VARIATION For your vegetarian option, use a 250 g (9 oz) pack of Quorn sausages. The Points per serving will be 2.

LAMB'S LIVER WITH BALSAMIC VINEGAR, SAGE AND APPLE

POINTS

per recipe: 7½ per serving: 3½

Serves 2
Preparation and cooking time: 25 minutes
Calories per serving: 270
Freezing: not recommended

This modern twist on an old favourite will ensure that you get your quota of iron and minerals. Serve on a bed of crushed swede.

350 g (12 oz) swede, peeled and diced
2 spring onions, chopped
2 tablespoons skimmed milk
1 teaspoon olive oil
200 g (7 oz) lamb's liver, cut into strips

1 small red-skinned apple, cored, and cut into 8 wedges
150 ml (¼ pint) unsweetened apple juice
1 tablespoon balsamic vinegar
3 fresh sage leaves, torn or ½ teaspoon dried
salt and freshly ground black pepper

1 Cook the swede in boiling salted water for 10 minutes. Drain, add the spring onions and milk. Cover and keep warm on the hob.
2 Heat a non-stick frying pan and add the oil and liver. Stir-fry for 1 minute. Add the apple wedges and stir-fry for a further minute. Stir in the apple juice, balsamic vinegar and sage. Cook over a high heat for 3–5 minutes until the liquid has nearly all evaporated.
3 Mash the swede. Season well. Spoon on to plates, and top with the liver and any remaining juices.

COOK'S TIP Balsamic vinegar has a uniquely intense flavour, and is comparable to a fine bottle of wine, sometimes in price too! However it's well worth investing in this highly valued product from Modena, Italy so that you can enjoy the intensity of just a few drops in dressings and sauces. Why not try drizzling a little over sliced strawberries or vanilla ice cream for a new and Point-free experience! Trust me, it's delicious.

VARIATIONS For a treat, you could try calves' liver in this recipe. Pork or turkey strips work well too. The Points per serving for pork would be 3. The Points per serving for turkey would be 2½.

Somerset Sausage Casserole: Cider and sausages taste wonderful in this warming casserole.

LAZY LAMB AND LENTILS

POINTS

per recipe: 13½   per serving: 3½

Serves 4
Preparation time: 10 minutes
Cooking time: 20 minutes
Calories per serving: 260
Freezing: recommended

I've called this dish 'lazy' since it needs so little preparation or attention.

350 g (12 oz) lean lamb, cut into 2 cm (³/₄-inch) pieces
1 onion, chopped
2 teaspoons garlic purée
2 teaspoons harissa (e.g. Bart's)
100 g (3½ oz) red lentils
200 g canned, chopped tomatoes
300 ml (½ pint) hot lamb or chicken stock
2 tablespoons chopped fresh parsley
salt and freshly ground black pepper

1 Dry-fry the lamb in a non-stick pan for 5 minutes, until lightly browned all over.

2 Add the onion, garlic and the harissa and continue to cook for a further 3–4 minutes. Add the lentils, tomatoes and stock. Bring to the boil, then cover and simmer for 20 minutes, or until the lentils are tender and the stock is nearly all absorbed.

3 Stir in the parsley. Check the seasoning, to taste. Serve.

WEIGHT WATCHERS TIP Lentils are a great source of protein and can be used in place of some of the meat in recipes. They are also delicious in soups too so it's a good idea to keep a packet of red lentils, which don't need pre-soaking of course, in your store cupboard.

Lamb Cutlets with Caramelised Minted Onions: The onions are deliciously sweet and sticky.

LAMB CUTLETS WITH CARAMELISED MINTED ONIONS

POINTS

per recipe: 11   per serving: 5½

Serves 2
Preparation and cooking time: 25 minutes
Calories per serving: 140
Freezing: not recommended

1 large red or white onion, sliced thinly
a pinch of dried rosemary
2 teaspoons mint jelly
4 lean lamb cutlets (75 g/2³/₄ oz each)
salt and freshly ground black pepper

1 Put the onion and rosemary in a small saucepan with 100 ml (3½ fl oz) water. Bring to a rapid boil. Cover and simmer for 10 minutes.

2 Preheat the grill.

3 Stir the mint jelly into the onions. Simmer, uncovered for 5 minutes, stirring occasionally. Season with salt and pepper.

4 Grill the cutlets for 2–3 minutes on either side. Serve with the sticky minted onions.

VARIATION For honey, thyme and balsamic onions, replace the mint jelly with 1 teaspoon runny honey and a few drops of balsamic vinegar. Add 1 teaspoon fresh chopped thyme.

GREEK-STYLE LAMB KEBABS

POINTS

per recipe: 24   per serving: 6

Serves 4

Preparation and cooking time:
30 minutes

Calories per serving: 265

Freezing: recommended

These kebabs are a cross between a burger and a sausage, so they should go down well with the family! Serve with a big tomato and onion salad and, if desired, some tzatziki (see Cook's tip). They are good served cold, too, so pop a couple in a lunch box with a big salad.

2 medium slices of white bread, crusts removed

450 g (1 lb) extra-lean minced lamb

1 small onion, grated

1 teaspoon garlic purée

1 teaspoon dried oregano

1 teaspoon dried mint

½ teaspoon paprika

1 teaspoon salt

1 egg, beaten

1 Preheat the grill and line the grill pan with aluminium foil.

2 Wet the bread under a running tap and squeeze out the excess water.

3 Using clean hands, mix together all the ingredients and bind them well. Divide the mixture into 12 even parts and make each into a short sausage.

Thread them on to metal skewers and place directly on to the grill pan.

4 Cook under a hot grill for 12–15 minutes, turning frequently to ensure even cooking.

COOK'S TIP To make tzatziki, stir 2 tablespoons chopped fresh mint and a 5 cm (2-inch) piece of cucumber, diced, into the Creamy Yogurt and Herb Dressing without the lime juice (see page 13). The Points per serving will remain the same.

VARIATION Thread tomato halves, pieces of green pepper and slices of courgettes between the lamb on the kebabs for a more substantial meal without adding any extra Points!

CREAMY LAMB, SPINACH AND CHICK-PEA STIR-FRY

POINTS

per recipe: 11½   per serving: 3

Serves 4

Preparation and cooking time:
30 minutes

Calories per serving: 250

Freezing: not recommended

This is good eaten with rice or warmed naan bread, adding the extra Points as necessary. Serve accompanied with extra fresh green vegetables – green beans or courgettes go well.

300 g (10½ oz) lean lamb, sliced into stir-fry strips

6 spring onions, trimmed and sliced

175 g (6 oz) baby spinach or kale or purple sprouting brocolli

175 g (6 oz) drained canned chick-peas

400 g (14 oz) canned chopped tomatoes

1 teaspoon cornflour blended in a little cold water

1 tablespoon fresh chopped chives or parsley

150 g (5½ oz) low-fat plain yogurt

salt and freshly ground black pepper

1 Dry-fry the lamb in a large non-stick frying pan for 4–5 minutes.

2 Add the spring onions, spinach or kale or brocolli, and stir-fry for a further 2 minutes.

3 Stir in the chick-peas, tomatoes, cornflour and chives or parsley. Season with a little salt and plenty of pepper. Cook for a further 10 minutes. Stir in the yogurt, just sufficiently to warm it through.

WEIGHT WATCHERS TIP A set of non-stick saucepans and a large frying pan or wok will help keep your Points down.

SPEEDY SHEPHERD'S PIE

POINTS

per recipe: 24½	per serving: 6

Serves 4
Preparation and cooking time:
30 minutes
Calories per serving: 355
Freezing: recommended

This is a foolproof way of ensuring the family will flock round on time for their meal. Serve with broccoli or courgettes.

500 g (1 lb 2 oz) large potatoes,
peeled and cubed
5 tablespoons semi-skimmed milk

450 g (1 lb) extra lean minced beef
150 ml (¼ pint) hot beef stock
300 ml tub of low-fat fresh
'Neapolitan-style' tomato pasta sauce
2 teaspoons Worcestershire sauce
salt and freshly ground black pepper

1 Cook the potatoes in boiling water for 12–15 minutes or until tender. Drain and mash with the milk and salt and pepper, to taste. Preheat the grill to medium.
2 Meanwhile, dry-fry the minced beef in a large non-stick saucepan for 5 minutes. Stir in the stock, pasta sauce and Worcestershire sauce. Simmer gently for 10 minutes until the mince is tender. Season to taste.

3 Spoon the mince into a shallow 1.2 litre (2-pint) flameproof dish and top evenly with the mashed potato. Place under the grill for 4–5 minutes, or until the topping is golden brown.

WEIGHT WATCHERS TIPS Most supermarkets now sell a core range of excellent pasta sauces. Look out for a Neapolitan-style sauce or tomato sauce, which is very low in fat.

Why not add 2 grated carrots (Points free!) or 125 g (4½ oz) frozen peas to the pasta sauce at stage 2? The Points per serving with frozen peas will be 6½.

Minced Beef, Beans and Pasta Bake: A nostalgic one-pot dish with appeal for all ages.

MINCED BEEF, BEANS AND PASTA BAKE

POINTS

per recipe: 21½	per serving: 5½

Serves 4
Preparation time: 5 minutes
Cooking time: 25 minutes
Calories per serving: 325
Freezing: recommended

Serve in warmed bowls with cauliflower or broccoli.

1 onion, chopped
350 g (12 oz) extra-lean minced beef
150 ml (¼ pint) beef stock
227 g can of chopped tomatoes
425 g (15 oz) canned Weight Watchers
from Heinz baked beans
2 teaspoons Worcestershire sauce
1 teaspoon dried mixed herbs
100 g (3½ oz) dried pasta twists
salt and freshly ground black pepper

1 Use a large non-stick saucepan to dry-fry the onion with the minced beef for 4–5 minutes until the meat becomes crumbly and browned.
2 Stir in the remaining ingredients. Bring to the boil, then cover and simmer gently for 20 minutes, until the pasta is cooked.
3 Season, to taste.

VARIATION For a vegetarian option, replace the minced beef with Quorn, and the beef stock with vegetable stock. Because Quorn does not have a lot of flavour on its own, try adding a teaspoon of chilli powder or medium curry powder with the Quorn at stage 1. The Points per serving will be 3½.

Speedy Shepherd's Pie: The all-time favourite ready in half the usual time!

Mexican Beef Tacos: Full of spicy beans and beef, these tacos make filling and fun finger food!

MEXICAN BEEF TACOS

POINTS
per recipe: 25½   per serving: 6½

Serves 4
Preparation time: 15 minutes
Cooking time: 15 minutes
Calories per serving: 430
Freezing: recommended for the
meat sauce

1 large onion, sliced

350 g (12 oz) extra-lean minced beef

1 teaspoon harissa or chilli paste
e.g. Bart's

½ teaspoon garlic purée

400 g (14 oz) canned, red kidney
beans, rinsed

400 g (14 oz) canned, chopped
tomatoes with herbs

12 taco shells

salt and freshly ground black pepper

1 quantity of Creamy Yogurt and Fresh
Herb Dressing (see page 13) excluding
the lime juice

2 limes, quartered, to serve

1 Place the onion, minced beef, harissa or chilli paste and garlic in a saucepan and dry-fry for 5 minutes, stirring frequently. If the mixture becomes too dry, add a few tablespoons of water just to moisten.
2 Add the red kidney beans and the chopped tomatoes. Season well and simmer uncovered, for 15 minutes.
3 Heat the grill to high and warm the tacos through for about a minute. Divide the beef mixture between the tacos. Top each one with the Creamy Yogurt and Herb Dressing. Serve with a lime wedge.

COOK'S TIP Taco shells are located alongside the ethnic section in the supermarket. Mexican ingredients are readily available, under the 'Old El Paso' brand or most supermarkets stock their 'own label'.

WEIGHT WATCHERS TIP Serve lots of shredded iceberg, tomato wedges and spring onions with these tacos, so that there is plenty to nibble on over this casual meal. Or bulk out the shells with a ready-prepared crunchy salad.

CHILLI BEEF WITH NOODLES

POINTS
per recipe: 9   per serving: 4½

Serves 2
Preparation and cooking time:
20 minutes
Calories per serving: 335
Freezing: not recommended

A little prime fillet of beef goes a long way in this quick dish. Why not treat yourself! This is a perfect impromtu meal for two.

1 teaspoon vegetable oil

175 g (6 oz) fillet of beef, sliced thinly

1 small onion, quartered, and the
layers separated

1 red pepper, de-seeded and cut into
bite-sized pieces

100 g (3½ oz) frozen broad beans

½–1 teaspoon chilli powder, or a few
drops of Tabasco sauce

½ teaspoon dried oregano

50 g (2 oz) dried tagliarini pasta or
fine egg noodles

200 ml (7 fl oz) hot beef stock

1 tablespoon sherry

1 tablespoon light soy sauce

200 g can of artichoke hearts in
water, drained and sliced lenthways
into 3, or canned celery hearts
(optional)

1 Heat the oil in a non-stick pan and stir-fry the beef for 2 minutes, until browned on all sides. Remove with a slotted spoon.
2 Add the onion quarters, red pepper and broad beans. Cook for 2 minutes, then stir in the chilli and oregano. Mix in the pasta or noodles, the stock, sherry and soy sauce. Cover and simmer for 4–5 minutes.
3 Return the beef to the pan together with the artichoke hearts, and simmer for 1 minute, to heat through. Serve.

COOK'S TIP If you have not tried artichokes, you really should and the canned version are much easier to use than the raw version! Mild yet succulent, they are very good in tomato-based dishes, salads and pasta dishes.

Vegetarian meals are extremely tasty, satisfying and easy to prepare so many people now find that a few of their weekly main meals are vegetarian. This chapter has some delicious, quick ideas for you to try out. All the recipes are nutritious with the required amount of protein to ensure that a vegetarian diet is a healthy one. And in addition to the meals in this chapter, don't forget to turn to the other chapters where you'll find vegetarian variations!

vegetarian .meals

GNOCCHI WITH A QUICK TOMATO SAUCE

POINTS

per recipe: 14	per serving: 3½

Ⓥ *Serves 4*
Preparation and cooking time: 30 minutes
Calories per serving: 230
Freezing: recommended for the sauce only

Gnocchi are Italian potato dumplings and they're ideal for a quick and filling supper.

400 g (14 oz) packet of chilled gnocchi
8 teaspoons parmesan cheese
a handful of torn basil leaves, to garnish

FOR THE TOMATO SAUCE
1 large onion, chopped finely
1 tablespoon tomato purée
2 × 400 g (14 oz) canned, chopped tomatoes with chilli
300 ml (½ pint) vegetable stock
1 teaspoon sugar
salt and freshly ground black pepper

1 Place all the ingredients for the sauce in a saucepan. Bring to the boil, and simmer uncovered for 20 minutes, until the liquid has been reduced to a thick pulpy sauce. Season to taste.
2 Meanwhile, cook the gnocchi, according to the pack instructions. Preheat the grill to high.
3 Spoon a little sauce in the base of four shallow, flameproof bowls. Add the drained gnocchi, and pour over the remaining sauce. Sprinkle on the cheese. Grill for 2 minutes, until the cheese turns golden brown.
4 Scatter the basil leaves over, and serve pronto!

COOK'S TIP This sauce is such a good base for so many dishes; it's excellent with grilled fish, chicken and pasta. Make up a batch and freeze handy portion sizes to use later.

WEIGHT WATCHERS TIP For special occasions, replace 150 ml (¼ pint) of the stock with red wine. Remember to add ½ Point per serving.

VARIATION Add 225 g (8 oz) chopped mushrooms, or 1 fiery hot chopped chilli and some chopped fresh coriander.

Gnocchi with a Quick Tomato Sauce: Ready-prepared Italian potato dumplings are so convenient.

Baked Beans and Potato Hash: The whole family will love this cheesy beany hash.

BAKED BEANS AND POTATO HASH

POINTS

per recipe: 21½   per serving: 5¼

Ⓥ *Serves 4*

Preparation and cooking time:
30 minutes
Calories per serving: 310
Freezing: recommended

---

600 g (1 lb 5 oz) potatoes, cut into
chunks

400 g (14 oz) leeks, sliced

2 garlic cloves, crushed or 2 teaspoons
garlic purée

200 g (7 oz) canned Weight Watchers
from Heinz baked beans

100 g (3½ oz) Gruyère cheese, grated

1 teaspoon dried sage

2 teaspoons vegetable oil

salt and freshly ground black pepper

1 Cook the potatoes in boiling water for 10 minutes. Add the leeks and cook for a further 5 minutes, or until the potatoes are tender. Drain and mash coarsely with the garlic. Stir in the beans, cheese and sage. Season to taste.

2 Heat the oil in a large frying pan, and press the potato mixture evenly over the base.

3 Cook for 7–8 minutes, or until crispy and golden on one side. Turn over and cook on the other side for a further 5 minutes. Cut into wedges and serve.

COOK'S TIP To help turn over the hash, invert the frying pan on to a large plate and then simply slide the hash back into the pan, browned side now facing up!

CREAMY POTATO, CAULIFLOWER AND CHICK-PEA KORMA

POINTS

per recipe: 14½   per serving: 3½

Ⓥ *Serves 4*

Preparation and cooking time:
30 minutes
Calories per serving: 305
Freezing: recommended

A mild and creamy vegetable curry, yet still perfectly warming for a chilly winter's evening. Serve with naan bread and pickles, adding the additional Points.

---

450 g (1 lb) new potatoes, scrubbed
and quartered

1 cauliflower, broken into florets

1 large onion, sliced

395 g jar of 98% fat-free Korma sauce
(e.g. Homepride)

400 g (14 oz) canned chick-peas, drained

100 g (3½ oz) baby spinach

4 tablespoons low-fat plain yogurt

2 tablespoons chopped fresh coriander

salt

1 Cook the potatoes in boiling water for 5 minutes. Add the cauliflower and onion. Cook for a further 10 minutes or until the vegetables are tender. Drain and return to the pan.

2 Stir in the Korma sauce. Heat through gently. Stir in the chick-peas and spinach. Cover and simmer for 10 minutes.

3 Season with salt. Stir in the yogurt and coriander. Serve.

LEEKS AND CANNELLINI BEANS WITH A GRILLED CHEESE SAUCE

POINTS

per recipe: 7½	per serving: 4

ⓥ *Serves 2*
Preparation and cooking time:
20 minutes
Calories per serving: 215
Freezing: not recommended

Tasty grilled cheese on top of creamy leeks and cannellini beans is so delicious. You can enjoy it piping hot, straight from the dish, and mop up the sauce with fresh granary bread, adding the extra Points. Serve with a tomato and onion salad.

10 baby leeks, trimmed and left whole, or 2 medium leeks, sliced thickly

300 g (10½ oz) canned cannellini beans, drained

2 teaspoons cornflour

75 g (2¾ oz) low-fat soft cheese with garlic and herbs

2 tablespoons chopped fresh chives

2 teaspoons freshly grated parmesan cheese

salt and freshly ground black pepper

1 Cook the leeks in boiling water for 5–7 minutes, until just tender. Drain thoroughly, reserving 150 ml (½ pint) of the cooking liquid. Arrange the leeks and cannellini beans in two individual shallow serving dishes.
2 Blend the cornflour with the cooking liquid, and return to the pan. Bring to the boil, stirring, until smooth and thickened. Add the soft cheese and chives. Season to taste. Simmer until the sauce is smooth.
3 Pour the sauce over the leeks and beans and sprinkle with parmesan cheese. Place under a preheated grill for 4–5 minutes until golden and bubbling.

VARIATIONS Replace the leeks with asparagus, or have a mixture of the two. For a non-vegetarian version, replace the beans with 150 g (5½ oz) wafer-thin smoked ham. The Points per serving will be 3.

BROAD BEAN AND LEEK TORTILLA

POINTS

per recipe: 14½	per serving: 3½

ⓥ *Serves 4*
Preparation and cooking time:
20 minutes
Calories per serving: 240
Freezing: not recommended

This is delicious with green vegetables and a fresh tomato salsa or salad.

250 g (9 oz) fresh or frozen broad beans

2 leeks, trimmed and sliced

2 courgettes, sliced thinly

1 tablespoon chopped fresh mint (or 1 teaspoon dried)

6 eggs, beaten

75 g (2¾ oz) low-fat (light) mozzarella cheese, cubed

salt and freshly ground black pepper

1 Blanch the beans, leeks and courgettes in a big pan of boiling water for 1 minute. Drain and refresh under cold running water. Drain thoroughly.
2 Dry-fry the vegetables with the mint in a large frying pan for 2–3 minutes. This will dry off any surplus moisture. Season the eggs, to taste, and then pour into the pan over the vegetables and cook gently for 6 minutes or until almost set.
3 Preheat the grill. Sprinkle the mozzarella over the top of the tortilla and brown under a hot grill for 2–3 minutes, until bubbling.
4 Cool slightly, before serving straight from the pan.

WEIGHT WATCHERS TIP Look out for reduced-fat cheeses, available at most supermarkets. If you cannot find light mozzarella, use a low-fat Edam or Cheddar instead.

VARIATION For a lightly spiced and fruity tortilla, replace the courgette with 1 chopped apple or 25 g (1 oz) dried apricots, chopped and added at stage two with 2 teaspoons of mild curry powder. The Points per serving will be the same.

Broad Bean and Leek Tortilla: Ideal for picnics and packed lunches when cold.

Jamaican Rum Pudding: If you can make this ahead of time, the gorgeous flavours will have time to develop.

delicious
desserts

On the Weight Watchers Programme, you can have your cake and eat it, but just remember, it's 'Everything in Moderation'! These scrumptious puddings are very satisfying and will easily help you to manage the desire for a little something sweet. And all are easy to prepare and need very little cooking so you can get them to the table quickly.

JAMAICAN RUM PUDDING

POINTS

per recipe: 23½   per serving: 6

Serves 4
Preparation time 10 minutes +
15 minutes chilling
Calories per serving: 310
Freezing: not recommended

This delicious version of trifle will go down a treat!

4 × 2 cm (³/₄ inch) slices of ready-made Jamaican Ginger cake (e.g. McVities)

227 g can of pineapple pieces in natural juice

1 small banana, sliced thinly

1 tablespoon rum

500 g carton of half-fat custard

150 g (5½ oz) Greek-style 0% yogurt

a pinch of ground cinnamon or ginger

1 Arrange the ginger cake between four individual sundae dishes. Drain the pineapple, reserving the juice, and place the pineapple pieces in the dishes together with the banana slices.

2 Spoon the rum and reserved pineapple juice over the fruits. Spoon the custard on top, to cover completely.

3 Spoon the yogurt on top of the custard. Chill for 15 minutes to allow the sponge to soak up the juice. Lightly sprinkle with ground cinnamon or ginger. Serve.

WEIGHT WATCHERS TIP

For special occasions, replace 3 tablespoons of pineapple juice with rum or brandy (in addition to the 1 tablespoon in the ingredients already!) Add ½ Point per serving.

Grilled Chocolate Peaches: Ripe and juicy peaches are ideal for this dessert.

GRILLED CHOCOLATE PEACHES

Ⓥ *Serves 4*

Preparation and cooking time: 10 minutes

Calories per serving: 135

Freezing: not recommended

---

2 fresh ripe peaches, halved and stoned

50 g (1¾ oz) plain chocolate, chopped into pieces

125 g (4½ oz) 0% fat Greek-style yogurt

4 teaspoons light or dark soft brown sugar

---

1 Preheat the grill to high. Place the peach halves in four ramekin dishes, cut side up.

2 Evenly divide the chocolate and place inside each hollow. Spoon on the yogurt to cover the peach completely. Evenly sprinkle the sugar over the surface.

3 Grill for 4–5 minutes, until the sugar has dissolved and the surface is bubbling. Serve immediately.

BAKED STRAWBERRY ALASKAS

Ⓥ *Makes 4*

Preparation and cooking time: 20 minutes

Calories per serving: 210

Freezing: not recommended

---

4 × 25 g (1¾ oz) slices of Swiss jam roll

1 ripe peach or nectarine, skinned and stoned

2 tablespoons sherry

250 g (9 oz) strawberries

1 egg white

50 g (1¾ oz) caster sugar

4 × 60 g (2 oz) scoops of Weight Watchers from Heinz Vanilla Iced Dessert

---

1 Preheat the grill to medium/high. Place the Swiss roll slices in the bases of four small ramekin dishes.

2 Mash or liquidize the peach or nectarine with the sherry. Thinly slice eight strawberries. Spoon the purée over the sponge bases and top with the sliced strawberries.

3 Make the meringue: whisk the egg white until stiff then whisk in the sugar, a little at a time, until the meringue becomes glossy.

4 Spoon a scoop of the iced dessert on top of the fruits, then swirl over the meringue. Make sure that the meringue forms a seal around the edge of each ramekin dish.

5 Flash under a hot grill just until the meringue is tinged golden brown. Serve immediately, topped with a whole strawberry.

VARIATION Replace the strawberries with fresh raspberries.

ALMOND MERINGUE PEACHES

Ⓥ *if using free-range eggs*

Serves 4

Preparation and cooking time: 20 minutes

Calories per serving: 165

Freezing: not recommended

This is a delicate and pretty dessert which is ideal for a special occasion.

---

425 g can of peach halves, drained

4 amaretti or macaroon biscuits

2 tablespoons Cointreau, Grand Marnier or sweet sherry

1 egg white

50 g (1¾ oz) caster sugar

15 g (½ oz) flaked almonds

---

1 Place the peaches, hollow side up, in a shallow flameproof dish to fit in the grill pan (remove the rack). Preheat the grill to low/medium.

2 Place a biscuit inside each peach hollow, then drizzle over the liqueur.

3 Whisk the egg white until stiff, then gradually whisk in the sugar. Spoon or pipe the meringue in a swirl over each peach.

4 Place under the grill and cook slowly for 3–4 minutes. Sprinkle on the almonds and continue to grill until the nuts become golden and the meringue is nicely coloured. Serve.

Baked Strawberry Alaskas: These can be kept in the freezer for up to 30 minutes before flashing them under the grill so they'll keep you as cool as the ice cream when entertaining!

CHERRY AND ALMOND OMELETTE

POINTS

per recipe: 24   per serving: 4

v *if using free-range eggs*
Serves 6
Preparation and cooking time:
25 minutes
Calories per serving: 230
Freezing: not recommended

Cherries and almonds conjure up memories of Italy with its lovely fruit orchards. This is delicious served with a scoop of Weight Watchers from Heinz Ice Cream, adding the extra Points.

25 g (1 oz) butter

2 × 425 g cans of pitted black cherries, drained

4 eggs, beaten

100 g (3¹/₂ oz) low-fat fromage frais

25 g (1 oz) caster sugar

25 g (1 oz) ground almonds

15 g (¹/₂ oz) flaked almonds

a dusting of icing sugar

1 Melt the butter in a large heavy-based frying pan. (The handle needs to be able to withstand the heat of the grill).

2 Heat the cherries in the butter for 3–4 minutes or until slightly softened.

3 Beat together the eggs, fromage frais, sugar and ground almonds. Pour over the cherries. Stir for the 3–4 minutes, then leave to lightly set for a further 5 minutes.

4 Sprinkle the flaked almonds over the top and place under a grill preheated to medium, to lightly toast the nuts. Serve warm, dusted with icing sugar.

Cherry and Almond Omelette: A sweet and satisfying dessert.

ORANGE JAFFA SURPRISE

POINTS

per recipe: 7   per serving: 3¹/₂

v *Serves 2*
Preparation time: 5 minutes +
10 minutes chilling
Calories per serving: 180
Freezing: not recommended

If you are a fan of Jaffa Cakes, you will find this idea a tasty way to make a couple go further! Leave this dessert to chill while the flavours are absorbed by the sponge base.

4 Jaffa cakes, diced

1 orange

150 g carton of low-fat ready-to-eat custard

1 Divide the cakes between two glass sundae dishes.

2 Peel and segment the orange over a bowl so that you can catch the juice. Chop the segments into pieces and scatter over the Jaffa cakes. Then pour on the reserved orange juice.

3 Spoon the custard evenly over the oranges. Chill for 10 minutes.

COOK'S TIP Individual 150 g cartons of low-fat ready-to-serve custard can be found in the grocery section.

PEAR BRUSCHETTA WITH CINNAMON SYRUP

Ⓥ *Serves 2*

Preparation and cooking time:
15 minutes
Calories per serving: 120
Freezing: not recommended

Serve with low-fat custard.

2 × 25 g (1 oz) slices of malt bread

227 g can of pear halves in natural
juice, drained and juice reserved

½ teaspoon caster sugar

½ teaspoon chopped nuts or flaked
almonds

1 teaspoon cornflour

a big pinch of ground cinnamon

1 Lightly toast the bread under a preheated medium grill on one side.
2 Slice the pear halves and then arrange in a fan-like shape on the untoasted side of each slice of bread. Sprinkle on half the sugar and all of the nuts. Grill under a medium heat until the sugar becomes lightly caramelised and the nuts turn golden.
3 Meanwhile blend the cornflour with a drop of the reserved juice, then stir in the remaining juice. Bring to the boil (either in a small saucepan or a jug in the microwave) until smooth and thickened. Stir in the remaining sugar and the cinnamon.
4 Drizzle the warm syrup over the grilled toasts. Serve immediately.

VARIATION Fresh ripe dessert pears can be used instead of canned. However, omit the cinnamon syrup and serve with 2 tablespoons of low-fat plain yogurt, sprinkled with cinnamon.

Pear Bruschetta: The malt bread becomes wonderfully gooey and caramelised when grilled.

STICKY TOFFEE FRUITS

Ⓥ *Serves 2*

Preparation and cooking time:
15 minutes
Calories per serving: 170
Freezing: not recommended

This is a good way to use up over-ripe fruit. You can use your favourite fruits in this recipe; pears, plums and pineapple are particularly good, especially with the thick and creamy fat-free Greek-style yogurt.

15 g (½ oz) butter

juice of 1 orange

1 apple, cored and sliced thickly

1 small banana, sliced thickly

a pinch of ground cinnamon

1 tablespoon soft light brown sugar

1 Melt the butter in a frying pan, add the orange juice and apple. Cook for 1 minute, then add the banana and cinnamon. Cook for a further 2 minutes until soft. Remove with a slotted spoon to two serving plates.
2 Increase the heat and add the sugar. Stir until dissolved, and allow the sauce to boil rapidly to reduce and become syrupy. Spoon over the warm fruits. Serve.

**Mango and
Raspberry
Stir-fry with
Lime and
Coconut Custard:
A tropical
sensation.**

MANGO AND RASPBERRY STIR-FRY WITH LIME AND COCONUT CUSTARD

POINTS

per recipe: 16   per serving: 8

Ⓥ Serves 2

*Preparation and cooking time:
15 minutes
Calories per serving: 330
Freezing: not recommended*

Serve warm (but not hot) to enjoy the flavours at their best.

15 g (½ oz) butter

1 ripe mango, peeled and sliced into strips

225 g (8 oz) fresh raspberries

200 ml (7 fl oz) reduced-fat coconut milk

2 teaspoons cornflour

1 teaspoon caster sugar

grated zest and juice of ½ lime

1 Melt the butter in a large frying pan and fry the mango and raspberries for 2 minutes or until the juices begin to run. Using a slotted spoon, transfer to 2 shallow bowls.

2 Heat all but 1 tablespoon of the coconut milk in the frying pan. Blend the remaining tablespoon with the cornflour, sugar and lime zest and juice. Stir this into the coconut milk in the frying pan and bring to the boil, stirring, until slightly thickened. (The sauce will will take on a pinkish colour from the raspberries.)

3 Serve warm, poured over the fruits.

WEIGHT WATCHERS TIP If you wish to omit the coconut sauce, and enjoy the fruits on their own, you can save 3 Points per serving.

VARIATIONS Bananas, pineapple, kiwi fruit and strawberries are all delicious cooked this way. Replace the raspberries with the equivalent weight of any of these fruits. Adjust the Points accordingly.

APPLE AND RASPBERRY DROP SCONES

POINTS

per recipe: 15½   per scone: 1½

*Makes 12
Preparation and cooking time:
20 minutes + 10 minutes standing
Calories per scone: 70
Freezing: not recommended*

Serve these sweet drop scones fresh from the pan. Enjoy with a spoonful of fat-free Greek-style yogurt.

100 g (3½ oz) self-raising flour

½ teaspoon ground cinnamon or allspice

2 tablespoons caster sugar

25 g (1 oz) butter

1 egg, beaten

125 ml (4 fl oz) skimmed milk

low-fat cooking spray

1 small dessert apple, peeled, cored and chopped finely

4 tablespoons fresh or frozen raspberries, lightly crushed

1 Sift the first three ingredients into a large bowl. Rub in the butter, make a well in the centre and beat in the egg and milk, to form a smooth batter. Leave to stand for 10 minutes.

2 Spray a non-stick frying pan with low-fat cooking spray and heat over a moderate heat. Stir the fruit into the batter.

3 Drop tablespoons of the batter into the pan and cook until the surface is covered with bubbles. Turn and cook on the other side until golden brown.

4 Keep the drop scones warm and moist in a clean folded tea towel while cooking the remainder. Serve warm.